THE BOSTON RED SOX

**MEMORIES AND
MEMENTOES OF
NEW ENGLAND'S TEAM**

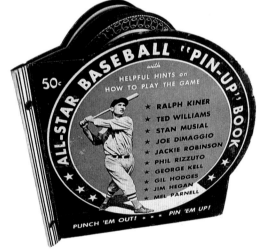

Text by Bruce Chadwick
Photography by David M. Spindel

ABBEVILLE PRESS • PUBLISHERS
New York • London • Paris

To my wife Barbara and children Jeff and Joyce for their patience and encouragement.   —D. S.

To Margie and Rory.   —B. C.

Library of Congress Cataloging-in-Publication Data
 Chadwick, Bruce.
    The Boston Red Sox : memories and
    mementoes of New England's team /
    by Bruce Chadwick : photography by
    David Spindel.
       p.   cm.
    Includes bibliographical references
    (p.   ) and index.
    ISBN 1-55859-242-3
    1. Boston Red Sox (Baseball team)—
    History.   I. Title.
 GV875.B62B487   1991
 796.357′64′0974461—dc20   91-32027
                                            CIP

Pages 2–3: The Red Sox, c. 1908 (see p. 21). Frontispiece: A closetful of Red Sox memorabilia. Title page: left, license plate from the '50s, and right, a pinup book (see p. 44). This page: a collection of Boston memorabilia from over the years. Page 7: Fenway plate from the '40s. Pages 8–9, left to right: ticket (see p. 59), Williams bat (p. 46), ball (p. 107), magazine (p. 23), Fisk (p. 98), banner (p. 85), megaphone (p. 115), box (p. 47), Tris Speaker (p. 18).

EDITOR: Constance Herndon
DESIGNER: Patricia Fabricant
PRODUCTION EDITORS: Philip Reynolds and
    Robin James
PRODUCTION SUPERVISOR: Hope Koturo

I fell in love with baseball and the Red Sox on the radio as a kid. I lived in a small town in Massachusetts far from Boston and every night I'd turn on the radio and tune it to the Red Sox games. The radio created a wonderful world for me, a foreign world way out there in the night of baseball and the Red Sox and that monument to all things that are good, the great Fenway Park. It was a beautiful world, a wonderful world out there, out there where the radio was coming from, and I couldn't wait to grow up and live in it.

—A. BARTLETT GIAMATTI

CONTENTS

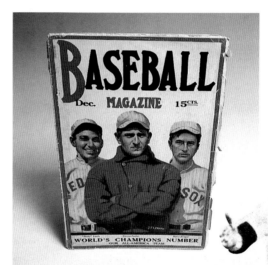

ACKNOWLEDGMENTS

We'd like to thank all the collectors, fans, and dealers, both kids and adults, who talked to us about their sports collections and allowed us to take photos of their memorabilia at stores, museums, and baseball card shows around the country. In particular, we are grateful to Frank Palmer and Mike Saunders of New Jersey and Richard Sachs of Massachusetts, who allowed us to spend far too much time in their homes. Our thanks go as well to Richard Johnson, director of the New England Sports Museum in Boston, for opening up his archives to us, and to Josh Evans, president of Lelands, the New York sports auction house, who helped us locate and photograph several collections.

We would also like to express our appreciation to the athletes, sports personalities, and broadcasters who talked to us, particularly Carl Yastrzemski, Mel Parnell, Mike Greenwell, Mel Allen, and Dick Radatz.

Finally, our special thanks to Constance Herndon, our editor, and Patricia Fabricant, our designer, who worked with us to turn a good book into a great one.

BRUCE CHADWICK AND DAVID SPINDEL

World Series memories—ticket stubs from the '46, '86, and '75 World Series.

THE EARLY DYNASTY
1901–1922

There is no team in baseball with a richer and more colorful history than the Red Sox and no city in the country with a more glorious baseball tradition than Boston. The town has one of the great ballparks in the world in venerable Fenway, the oldest, oddest, and most wonderful stadium in the land. The Red Sox have had some of the greatest players in the game, baseball giants like Cy Young, Smoky Joe Wood, Tris Speaker, Ted Williams, Bobby Doerr, and Carl Yastrzemski. Today the Red Sox have some of the game's top players, too, with people like Roger Clemens, Wade Boggs, and Mike Greenwell. Win or lose, the team has been involved in many of sports' great controversial moments, from Fred Snodgrass's dropped fly ball in the 1912 World Series to the late-season miracle of the Sox's pennant grab in '67 to Carlton Fisk's twelfth-inning home run in the sixth game of the '75 Series. The Red Sox have brought fans great triumphs and great failures, first place flourishes and last place finishes, early World Series glory and recent World Series heartbreak. And, for fans young and old, a million memories.

What makes the Red Sox so unique, different from just about every other team in the Major Leagues, is its regional roots. This is a team for all of New England, not just the city limits of Boston and the farthest stops of the MTA.

Cy Young arrived in Boston in 1901 and presented the Red Sox with instant credibility by winning thirty-three games, followed by thirty-two in 1902. He went on to win 511 games, a feat that is still unmatched.

13

Jimmy Collins was the player/manager of the Red Sox from 1901 to 1906, serving only as manager in 1907 before retiring.

In San Francisco, there are Giants fans on the peninsula where the city sits, but millions of A's fans right across the bay in Oakland. In New York there are lots of Yankees fans, but millions of Mets fans, too. But in New England, whether it's ski instructors in Killington, bartenders in Providence, or kids playing Little League in Bangor, everybody, but everybody, loves the Red Sox. It is the only truly regional team in America.

Boston is a city where baseball reaches back to the very roots of the game itself, back to when U. S. Grant was president. When the National League was formed in 1876, the Boston Baseball Club (later the Braves) was one of its first entries. The club played through the turn of the century and became, with the New York Giants and the Cincinnati Reds, a pillar of American baseball. By the time Ban Johnson decided to begin the upstart American League in 1901, baseball was already well established around the Boston Common. And so the new league, eager to introduce franchises in cities where National League teams had proved the game could flourish, turned to Boston.

Now, the league's management certainly couldn't assure its teams' success on the field, but it could through manipulation assure box office success. With open wallets as their weapons, the American League helped its teams raid National League teams and pirate away top stars.

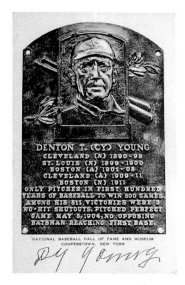

An autographed Cy Young Hall of Fame card.

14

Huntington Avenue Grounds was the first home of the Red Sox, and on this enormous field the team won baseball's very first World Series in 1903.

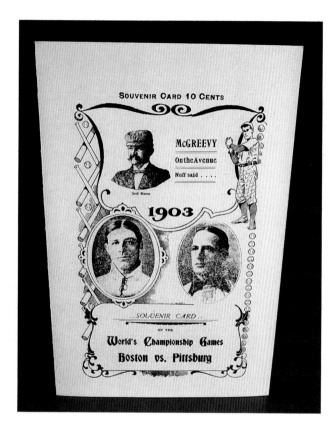

A rare souvenir card
from the first World
Series in 1903, in
which the Red Sox
defeated Pittsburgh.

Poster of the 1904
Boston team, win-
ners of the very first
World Series over
Pittsburgh the sum-
mer before.

16

An old bottle bat used by the team around 1905. This shape was thought to be more effective because players could get a good grip on the handle, but physicists later proved that thin handles produced greater bat speed.

A specially mono-grammed Red Sox straight razor from about 1907.

The Red Sox, known as the Pilgrims back then, were one of the most successful teams at this. Their first lineup included Buck Freeman from Washington, D.C., Freddy Parent from Saint Louis, Jimmy Collins, the slugging star from Louisville (who would also serve as player/manager), and Chick Stahl, from the cross-town National League Boston Beaneaters (later the Braves). The biggest star they secured, though, the man who would quickly bring the fans unexpected glory, was the best pitcher in baseball, Cy Young.

That very first season, the Pilgrims finished a respectable second to the Chi-cago White Sox (just four games out) and Cy Young stunned the youthful American League by winning thirty-three games. In 1902, red-hot Young won thirty-two games and the Pilgrims finished third behind the Philadelphia Athletics and the Saint Louis Browns.

In 1903, only their third season, the Pilgrims took the American League pen-nant behind the solid pitching of a staff with three 20-game winners: Young (28–9), Long Tom Hughes (20–7), and Bill Din-neen (21–11). Owner Henry Killilea met with National League Pittsburgh Pirates' owner Barney Dreyfuss in August and

With his fluid swing, Tris Speaker established the fourth-highest batting average on record, hitting .344 lifetime and twice hitting over .380. In the field Speaker revolutionized the game by playing a very shallow center, which allowed him to grab line drives and one-hop drives to throw runners out at first. He holds the all-time record for outfielder putouts.

decided that if their two front runners finished first they would play each other in a "world championship" series.

That very unofficial series became the first World Series. Set for nine games, it opened in Boston at the Huntington Avenue Grounds with 16,242 fans on hand to watch Cy Young battle National League ace Deacon Phillippe. The Pirates battered Young early and took the first game, 7–3. They kept winning and held a 3–1 series lead before Young and Dinneen found their rhythm and shut down Pittsburgh in the last four games to give Boston its first world championship, five games to four.

The Pilgrims took the pennant again in 1904 behind more sound pitching (Young was 26–16, Dinneen was 23–14, and newcomer Jesse Tannehill was 21–11). They squeaked into first place by beating Jack Chesbro and the Yankees on the last weekend of the year, setting the stage for an almost ninety-year Boston–New York rivalry, one of American sports' finest. There was no second World Series, though, because the incensed president of the New York Giants, John T. Brush, refused to play, claiming that the National League was far too superior to meet a minor-league team like Boston. So the Pilgrims simply claimed their second world championship by default.

Boston slid to fourth place in 1905 and remained stuck in the middle of the American League for several years. Then in 1909, the erstwhile Pilgrims, by now officially the Red Sox, signed one of the game's great players, Tris Speaker, who promptly hit .309. They also signed an unlikely young pitcher named Joseph Wood, who came to them from a midwest women's team called the Bloomer Girls, where he was a ringer. While no one expected much, that first season in Boston Wood posted a very respectable 11–7 record and the Sox finished third. The 1910 season saw the arrival of Harry Hooper, now in the Hall of Fame, and Duffy Lewis. Along with Speaker, the three immediately became the finest defensive outfield in the world. Nevertheless, Boston finished fourth that year and in 1911 dropped to fifth.

The next year everything started to change, beginning in April with the opening of Fenway Park (named because it was located in a section of town known as the Fenways and because it sat on land owned by the Fenway Realty Company). The Red Sox had a new park and they had a new manager, a man named Jake Stahl who had previously stumbled as Boston's manager in 1905 and 1906. Unlike most managers, who worked for the paycheck, Stahl was

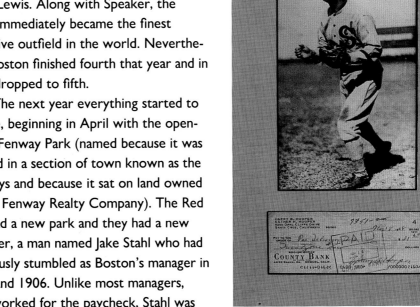

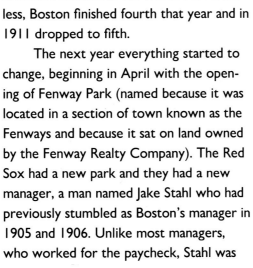

wealthy. He played baseball for the fun of it and managed for the same reason.

Putting '05 and '06 behind him, Stahl drove the Sox from a fifth-place finish in 1911 to first and a pennant in 1912. After the next season he left the team following dissension on the club. But 1912, the centerpiece in his brief career—that was something else. Tris Speaker hit a sizzling .383. Speaker's roommate Joe Wood, known as Smoky Joe because of his blazing fastball, had perhaps the finest year any pitcher ever enjoyed, winning sixteen consecutive games, finishing with a 34–5 record, and posting a 1.91 ERA.

Wood wasn't the only hot pitcher out there that year; he was just the hottest. After Cy Young's retirement in 1911 at age forty, the premier pitcher of the times was the Washington Senators' Walter Johnson. He, too, won sixteen in a row in 1912—until he came to Boston. When

Wood and Johnson finally faced each other, the local Boston papers ran comparison charts of both men the way they did with prize fighters. So many thousands of people jammed Fenway that the police let hundreds sit on the ground just behind the foul lines and more than three thousand sat on the outfield grass behind ropes. Cops had to clear an area in the middle of the pressing crowds so that Wood and Johnson had room to warm up before the game. It was one of baseball's greatest days, although not for Johnson. Like everyone before him, he was stopped cold by Smoky Joe Wood.

"Can I throw harder than Joe Wood?," he answered a reporter. "Listen, my friend, there's no man alive who can throw harder than Smoky Joe Wood."

Led by Speaker and Hooper, the 1912 team and those for six years after were superb defensive clubs. Speaker revolutionized the game by playing a very shallow centerfield. This enabled him to toss out runners consistently at first base—unheard of today—and to double up runners at second. But he was rangy enough to fall back quickly on balls hit over his head. According to Wood, Speaker had great instincts that would send him run-

The Red Sox on the road around 1908, accompanied by dozens of fans who traveled from Boston to cheer them on.

21

ning to where the ball would fall before he ever heard the crack of the bat. But Smoky Joe also claimed that Hooper, who was always overshadowed by Speaker, was just as good.

From 1912 to 1918, Boston would dominate baseball, winning pennants in 1912, 1915, 1916, and 1918, and the World Series in each of those years. In addition to Wood, who posted a 115–57 record, the Red Sox later signed pitchers Dutch Leonard and Carl Mays. Speaker and Hooper were spectacular fielders and consistent hitters, Speaker hitting .344 lifetime and Hooper hitting .281. Each is now in the Hall of Fame.

Amid all this success unfolded the sad and courageous story of Smoky Joe Wood. In the spring after his miraculous 1912 season, Wood fell on his pitching hand, breaking his thumb. The hand was never the same again and the more he exercised it the worse it got. Today, with advanced surgery, Wood might have missed a month

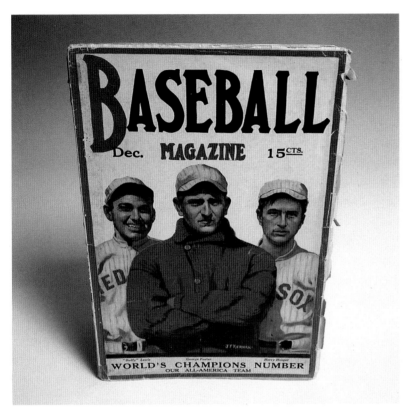

posted a .282 lifetime average but could also hit for power. One of the greatest days any player has ever had came in 1918 when early in the game Joe Wood hit a home run against the Yankees to keep the Sox in a tight game and returned with another titanic home run in the eighteenth inning to win it. Wood's transformation and return from oblivion was certainly remarkable, and some insist that his story was the basis for Bernard Malamud's book *The Natural,* made into a Robert Redford movie that is considered one of the finest ever made on the game.

The Sox were winners and they were exciting winners. Players did the unexpected—for example, in 1912 light-hitting Hugh Bradley, whose idea of power was a liner to the mound, hit the first home run in spanking new Fenway Park, his only

A 1916 *Baseball* magazine issue with the world champ Sox on cover.

and returned to the mound as good as new, but in 1913 nothing could be done. His arm hurt continually as he struggled to an 11–5 mark in 1913, followed by 9–3 in 1914 and 14–5 in 1915. At times the pain was so bad that in movie theaters he could not lift his arm over the seat, and at the end of the 1915 season he was forced to quit baseball. Unwilling to live in retirement, however, Wood returned to the game several years later as an outfielder and became one of the best in baseball. He

Old copies of *Baseball* magazine with issues devoted to the crosstown Boston Braves and the Royal Rooters, a fan club.

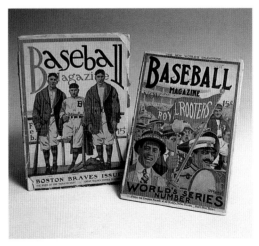

Young Babe Ruth was the finest hurler in the game, winning twenty-three games in one year. During a typical game in 1916, he went three for four at the plate with a home run and a double, and also pitched a three-hit shutout. If he started to lose, his hitting was too good to take him out of the game —instead he'd be moved to first base or right field so that his bat would remain in the order.

home run of the year. Another surprising force on the team was Rough Bill Carrigan, a sturdy catcher who let no one intimidate him. The first few times he played Ty Cobb and the Detroit Tigers, Carrigan, like others, shied away from tagging Cobb out on a slide at the plate because Cobb slid into catchers with his sharpened spikes, often slashing their arms and legs open. But Carrigan finally found a solution. One day Cobb, spikes high and flying, slid in as usual. Deftly Carrigan stepped out of the way of the spikes and then, intent on making a putout, punched Cobb right in the face as hard as he could with the hand that held the ball. Cobb was out at the plate and out cold, carried out of Fenway on a stretcher. He menaced Bill Carrigan no more.

The Red Sox had great players and wonderful balance in those years, but their anchor was an amazing young player out of a Baltimore home for boys. George Herman Ruth arrived in 1914 as a part-time pitcher and exploded onto the main stage in 1915, winning eighteen games on the mound and hitting .315 at the plate in forty-two games. Manager Carrigan (if he was tough enough for Ty Cobb he was tough enough for the front office) didn't know what to do with him—use him as the game's best pitcher, or as the game's best hitter?

The Babe was phenomenal. In 1916

he set baseball on its ear with a 23–12 record and a 1.75 ERA, and at the plate he hit .272. The next year he posted a 24–13 record and batted .325. In 1918, the year of Boston's last world championship, the Babe pitched less often (13–7) and played the field more (ninety-five games). He hit .300 and became something of a slugger

Ruth the slugger emerged slowly, hitting .272 in 1916, .325 in 1917, and .300 in 1918 with eleven home runs in ninety-five games. He played 130 games in 1919 and set baseball on its ear by smashing a record twenty-nine home runs.

Carl Mays was a fine pitcher who won twenty-one games in 1918, but the next season he had a falling out with owner Harry Frazee. Instead of reconciling, an angered Frazee sold him to the Yankees, who asked if anyone else was available. . . .

To raise money for his Broadway shows, owner Harry Frazee then sold Babe Ruth to the Yankees in 1920 for $100,000, a disastrous move that he followed by shipping out another dozen stars over the next few years. This generosity toward New York destroyed the Red Sox, a crime for which Boston has never forgiven Frazee.

CARL MAYS

with eleven home runs. In 1919 he pitched even less (8–5) but he turned baseball upside down at the plate, where he crashed a record twenty-nine home runs in 130 games.

Harry Hooper played with Ruth all those years and knew the Babe before he put on all that weight. "I still can't believe what I saw," he told writer Lawrence Ritter, "this nineteen-year-old kid, crude, poorly educated, gradually transformed into the idol of American youth and the symbol of baseball the world over."

The Boston fans were in love with their team and in love with Ruth. As the Roaring Twenties approached, the Red Sox's glory was only beginning to unfold. Boston would have the best team in the country, that much was clear, and owner Harry Frazee would become the most famous owner in the game.

But in the middle of the 1919 season, Carl Mays, who had won twenty-one games the year before, feuded with Boston management. Rather than give in to Mays's demands, Frazee sold him to the Yankees, probably using some of the money for the musicals he backed in New York—theater was his passion. Sox fans should have heard the creaking timbers of a roof about to fall in. On January 9, 1920, Frazee sold Ruth to the Yankees for $100,000, an act outraged fans called the "crime of the century."

The sale of Ruth crushed fan morale in Boston. To make matters worse, Frazee soon sold the Yankees four of his top pitchers, Sad Sam Jones, Herb Pennock, Waite Schoolboy Hoyt, and Bullet Joe Bush, along with Wally Schang and Mike McNally. Boston had the best players in baseball—the problem was they were all playing for the Yankees.

As for Frazee, although he villified himself thoroughly in Boston, the Sox's owner did endear himself to theatergoers by investing all those ill-gotten Yankee gains into several musicals, among them the hit *No, No, Nanette.* But baseball fans weren't charmed. By 1922, following Frazee's crazy trades, the Red Sox had stumbled into last place. They would not win a pennant again until 1946 and have yet to win another World Series. What started as a great dynasty in 1903 and seemed destined to become legend had collapsed after just fifteen years. The Sox would not rise again until two world wars were fought.

This 1918 *New York Times* sports page, with a majestic picture of young pitcher Babe Ruth, heralds the coming World Series against the Cubs, the last Boston would win.

THE HUNGRY YEARS
1922–1939

Everybody was howling about the rape of the Red Sox, as it quickly became known. No one was angry at Jacob Ruppert, the Yankee owner who did the buying. Everyone's anger was directed at Frazee, who did the selling.

"Boston last season reached the fruits of four years' despoilation by the New York club," wrote the editors of the *Reach Guide,* the *Sports Illustrated* of the era. "And for the second time in American League base-ball history, this once great Boston team, now utterly discredited, fell into last place, with every prospect of remaining in that undesirable position indefinitely."

But the Sox weren't discredited enough, for Frazee the trader—or was it traitor?—had one more great deal up his sleeve. In 1922 he ruined Sox fans' winter by trading ten-year veteran lefthander Herb Pennock to the Yankees along with George Pipgras, for a carload of unknowns. Frazee argued that Pennock only posted a 10–17 record the previous season. So just to show his ex-boss the score, Pennock promptly went 19–6 for the Yankees in 1923.

More eager for opening nights than opening days, entrepreneur Frazee plunged into the New York theater world and sold the club in 1923 to Bob Quinn, former general manager of the Saint Louis Browns, and

A big finish for a big swing from Jimmy Foxx, who came to the Sox from the A's in 1935 and helped turn the club around.

29

course there were more of those brilliant Red Sox trades. The worst was the deal that sent pitcher Red Ruffing to (who else?) the Yankees, in exchange for slugger Cedric Durst. The dangerous Durst immediately hit .240 and retired, while Ruffing posted a sparkling 15–5 record for the Yankees and went on to be enshrined in baseball's Hall of Fame.

The Red Sox were the disgrace of the American League. They had no players, no promise, and no future. In the twelve seasons between 1922 and 1933, they finished in last place nine times.

But the entire history of the team, and the city, began to turn around in 1933 when a young entrepreneur named Thomas Austin Yawkey bought the Sox. Yawkey was from a baseball family. His uncle owned the Detroit Tigers from 1904 to 1907 and the game was in Tom's blood. He was a respected businessman in 1933, a sharp dresser, a quiet gentleman, and he was just thirty years old. He knew—all of Boston and New England knew—that he had a rare opportunity, the opportunity to remold and reshape the Boston Red Sox completely and to run the club for a lifetime. He could bring in a new general manager, a new manager, new coaches, and new players. He was the sole owner and the team was all his. Boston fans expected plenty from the innocent-looking young

Tom Yawkey decided to lavish his inherited wealth on his baseball team, the Red Sox. He bought the team in 1933 for $1.5 million, renovated Fenway in 1934, and spent millions more in the forty-four years he ran the team as sole owner.

millionaire Winslow Palmer. They had a team, a stadium, money, and, as all Red Sox fans know, nothing but bad luck. Palmer, whose money had been counted on to buy talent, started off the new regime badly by dying less than two years after he became part owner of the team. Quinn then ran into what seemed to be years of rainy weather. Every time he had a good weekend series with a top team lined up, Boston got rain. It didn't seem to rain anywhere else in the world in those years, only in Boston. His pennant hopes, and his bank account, drowned in rain. And of

Jean Yawkey watched the successes and failures of the Red Sox at her husband's side through four decades. On his death in 1977 she took over and remains chairwoman of the board. In 1978 she sold a large interest in the club to a group headed up by Haywood Sullivan, now general partner and club president.

man with the short-cropped hair and the quiet, elegant wife.

Yawkey emptied his very deep pockets into the ballclub in 1933, and in 1943, and in 1953, and in 1963. He never held back in his love for the Red Sox or his willingness to spend money to acquire the talent he needed. In all the years he owned the team, nobody took more pride in the Red Sox than Tom Yawkey, and no one hurt as much that there was never a world championship. Whatever happened to the Red Sox from 1933 on, the ups and downs, triumphs and tragedies, it was all thanks to

Yawkey. His critics charged that he held on to managers too long, that he was a bad judge of front-office talent, didn't know how to get needed pitchers, and hired too many men because they were nice guys, not baseball guys. Maybe they were right. The old timers shake their heads, though, and they remind you . . . from 1922 to 1933, nine of twelve last-place finishes. Whatever else Yawkey did, he moved the Red Sox out of the basement and up into the parlor suites.

"I think that as much as he saw himself as the man who owned the team, to most he *was* the team," said the late Commissioner of Baseball Bart Giamatti. "Yawkey, in his moves over the years, really established the team that the Sox became and their place in history. I can't think of another owner in baseball so closely identified with a team."

The first order of business for the dapper, well-dressed new owner was a $750,000 reconstruction of Fenway. Yawkey correctly felt that a spruced up Fenway would make fans happy, but that a talented general manager and field manager would make them even happier. So he hired Hall-of-Famer Eddie Collins as his first general manager, followed by Joe Cronin to manage the team. Collins was not only a man of supreme integrity—one of the few Chicago White Sox who gam-

31

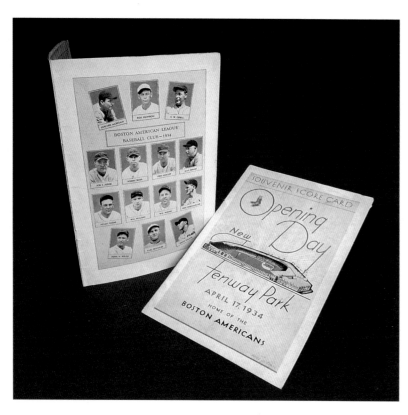

Scorecard from reopening game at Fenway in 1934 following major renovation by Tom Yawkey.

blers didn't consider approaching in 1919 for the World Series fix—but he had played the game for twenty-five years and understood the ballplayers. He had also put in a considerable amount of time in management while finishing out his playing days, serving as player-manager for the White Sox in 1925 and 1926. Fired because of two fifth-place finishes, Collins took a train to Philadelphia and became a third base coach for the A's managing genius, Connie Mack. The hard-working Collins helped the A's win three straight pennants. He turned down other managing jobs because he was convinced that Mack, then sixty-seven, would retire and he would replace him. But he reconsidered when Yawkey made his offer—a wise move since Mack managed for twenty-one more years.

Once with the Sox, Collins urged Yawkey to hire Joe Cronin away from Washington as field manager of the team. Like Collins, Cronin was a player-manager who knew his athletes. He knew his managing too, having led the Senators to a pennant in his first season, 1933. He arrived in Boston as player-manager in 1935 to begin one of the most distinguished careers in sports. The handsome shortstop with the Homeric jaw continued his Hall of Fame playing career (he would hit .301 lifetime) and settled in as manager.

Red Sox cap.

With Yawkey and Collins, Cronin would make changes that would turn Boston's fortunes around. Following his eleven years as a manager, he then became general manager and later president of the American League.

Whatever faith owner Yawkey needed in his ballclub arrived in 1935, Cronin's first season, when the team beat the hated Yankees five straight—and at Fenway in front of a roaring crowd. That season Collins brought in a variety of new players to help the Red Sox climb out of the second division, some though not all of whom contributed significantly.

The chief acquisition was ace pitcher

An early Red Sox program from 1934. Rooms at luxury hotels advertised in the program charged a heady $3 per night.

Opposite, Lefty Grove taught himself pitching by throwing rocks as a kid, eventually becoming the greatest lefthanded hurler to play the game. Even though he didn't make the majors until age twenty-five, he won three hundred games and fashioned eight twenty-win seasons including a 31–4 record in 1931 for the Philadelphia A's.

Right, Burly Joe Cronin was hired as manager by Tom Yawkey to bring stability to the Red Sox. Before becoming a manager the barrel-figured Cronin had been a great player, making the All Star team at shortstop seven times, winning the MVP crown in 1930, and later being named to the Hall of Fame. As manager, he took a terrible team and built it into a contender by the end of the decade.

Lefty Grove. Before moving to Boston he had been a star for nine years in Philadelphia, winning twenty-four games in 1933. As a veteran pitcher he was much older than his teammates in Philadelphia and Boston (he didn't even get to the majors until he was 25), but Grove's age did not hinder him. When he arrived in Boston, he and Collins realized his arm was not nearly as strong as it had been. Lefty, using all of his wiles, then concentrated on pitching finesse rather than throwing speed and won twenty games in 1935. He continued to play until 1941, winning his three hundredth game in his very last outing.

The Sox also acquired Max Bishop, but he fizzled and shortly retired. Also from the A's they got Rube Walberg, a

Left, a mug from Fenway.

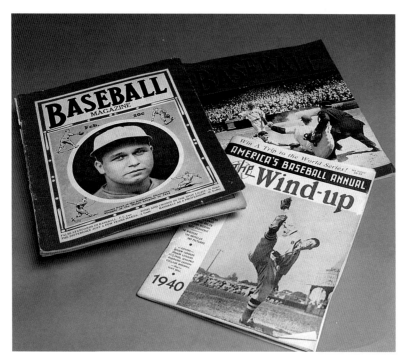

pitcher who worked mostly in relief through 1937. Heinie Manush came in from Washington and hit .291 in 1936 but was soon traded. The Boston management did come up with one winner in their fishing expedition, however. Hall-of-Famer Jimmie Foxx arrived in 1935 and promptly smacked forty-one home runs, 143 RBIs, and averaged .338 in his first season with the club. Of Foxx's 534 lifetime home runs, 218 were with the Red Sox, and in six seasons with Boston he hit .321 with 774 RBIs.

These 1930s magazines feature Red Sox slugger Jimmy Foxx and pitcher Lefty Grove.

Boston slugger Jimmy Foxx on the cover of *Who's Who in Baseball*, 1939.

A fascinating poster featuring players from the '36 team. "After waiting 18 years," it says, "Boston now has pennant hope."

AFTER WAITING EIGHTEEN YEARS — BOSTON NOW HAS PENNANT HOPE

All the hard work and all the acquisitions paid off. Boston finished sixth in 1936 and fifth in 1937. In both 1938 and 1939 the club came in second, only trailing the hated Yankees. Yawkee and Cronin had completely turned around the fortunes of the team and won back the hearts of the Boston fans.

The traditional heavy wool Red Sox warm-up jacket.

FENWAY

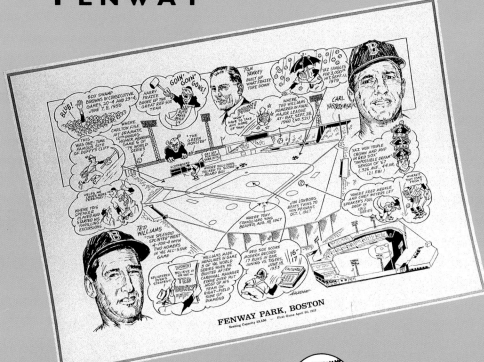

Drawing illustrating the glorious history of Fenway and the Red Sox. These blotter-sized posters were created for a dozen different ballparks.

Fenway isn't old, it's sacred. For the city or state to tear it down would be like the government of Greece tearing down the Parthenon.

—DICK JOHNSON,
executive director of the
New England Sports Museum

I would stand on first and look around, and you were so close that you could actually see the people. I don't mean see the *crowd,* but see the individuals and their features. It made it more personal, playing for each person, not just some big crowd.

—CARL YASTRZEMSKI, Boston Red Sox

Fenway silk scarf.

Above, a packed Fenway on a summer afternoon, and below, a plate from the Fenway bullpen signed by Ted Williams, along with a Williams glove and ball.

When I was seven years old my father took me to Fenway Park for the first time, and as I grew up I knew that as a building it was on the level of Mount Olympus, the Pyramid at Giza, the nation's capitol, the czar's Winter Palace, and the Louvre—except, of course, that it was better than all those inconsequential places.

—the late A. BARTLETT GIAMATTI, Commissioner of Baseball and lifelong Red Sox fan

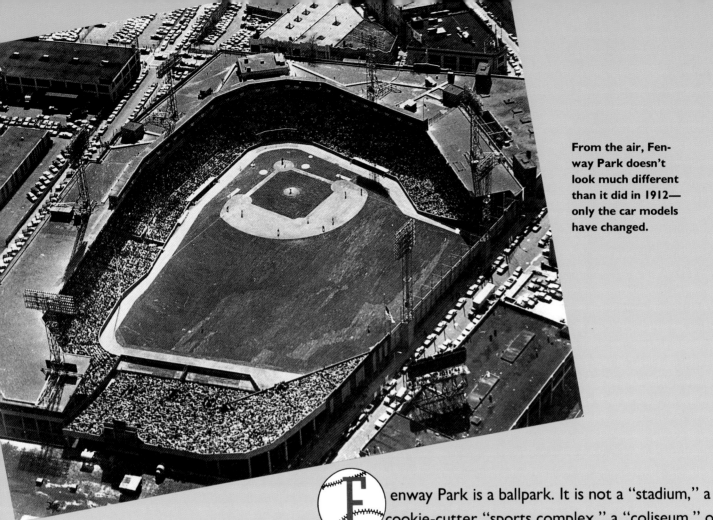

From the air, Fenway Park doesn't look much different than it did in 1912—only the car models have changed.

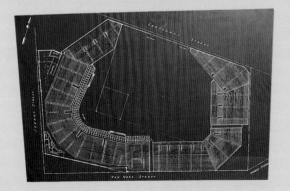

One of the original architectural plans for Fenway.

enway Park is a ballpark. It is not a "stadium," a cookie-cutter "sports complex," a "coliseum," or an athletic field named after some local big shot. It is a ballpark in the traditional sense of the word, a park not so much surrounded by Boston as embraced by it. Fenway is not bordered by parking lots, water fountains, or lawns, like "stadiums," but by city streets and neighborhoods. It has the Green Monster in left field not because someone wanted a high left field wall but because the wall had to protect Landsdowne Street behind it. It has no upper deck because nobody ever needed one. The seats are very close to the field because in 1912 they were very close to the field.

The beauty of Fenway has always been its intimacy. People from all over the country have come to Fenway and marveled at how close they sat to the infield or how close the seats are down the foul lines. They say how wonderful it is to sit there on the first base side and look up to see the big Moosehead Beer and Citgo signs over the Wall, and they talk about how you can "hear" the game as well as see it.

This is the oldest major-league ballpark in America, the field where Tris Speaker played shallow center, where Babe Ruth won ninety-four games as a pitcher and began his legendary career as a slugger, and where Ted Williams became the last man to hit .400. This is a park where no one, absolutely no one, complains about the pillars blocking a view, where all the fold-down seats are still made of wood, and where the security people don't confiscate beach balls tossed around the bleachers. No matter where you go in Fenway there's a box for the Jimmy Fund, and the huge open gaps in the grandstand walls make the game a part of the neighborhood.

Fenway is a ballpark surrounded by side streets that become carnivals on game day, with dozens of souvenir stands and stores selling baseball cards. Cabs race up and down streets, long lines of charter buses hug the sidewalk, and people scurry about looking for tickets. It's a ballpark full of noise. Its small dimensions mean that the screams of fans fly quickly through the air and down to the field, the roar turning into a crescendo.

The city of Boston symbolizes all that is old and traditional and good in America, and Fenway Park embodies Boston.

The numbers 9 (Williams) and 8 (Yaz) from the Fenway scoreboard, signed by the players.

TED WILLIAMS
THE EARLY '40s

From the first day he put on the Boston uniform in 1939, Ted Williams was a star. His goal was always the same and he quickly announced it to anyone who would listen: he wanted to be the greatest batter in the history of the game.

Good idea, but ideas don't have to play ball. Hitting a ninety-m.p.h. fastball may be the toughest single act in sports. A player struggles to become a great power hitter, a great average hitter, a great clutch hitter, or a great fielder. But to be all these things, and be them consistently over a long career, is unheard of. Ty Cobb was a great average hitter (.367) but he had no power. Yankee Hall-of-Famer Earle Coombs hit .325 lifetime but only cracked sixty-nine home runs in eleven years. Other great ball-players perform consistently well without being spectacular, among them the immortal Harry Hooper, star of the early Red Sox, who hit only .281 lifetime. Then there are players who start slowly and build to a sizzle, players with great rookie years who then fade, like Joe Charboneau of the Cleveland Indians, and sluggers who end their careers in the .220 society.

And then there was Ted Williams. Teddy Ballgame has become such a legend over the years that today we forget why he grew to such mythic proportions. Here was a great power hitter who slammed 521 home runs and still hit .344 lifetime. Here was a man who had the second-highest

Ted Williams as a raw, rail-thin rookie.

43

A Williams glove and its original box, now owned by Mike Saunders. "To me he was, bar none, the greatest baseball player ever," said Saunders, the trainer for the New York Knicks.

slugging average in history and also rapped out 2,654 hits. Here was a man who was famous for his home run clouts each season (forty-three in his best year and a final home run in his very last at bat), and still won batting titles in six different years. He hit .304 in eighteen All Star games against the best pitching in the world. He even hit a home run off Rip Sewell's immortal ephus pitch. The man never batted below .318, he hit thirty or more homers in eight years, and he had a hundred or more walks eleven times. In addition, Williams was named MVP twice (and should have been twice more), won two Triple Crowns, hit .388 at age thirty-nine, and won his final batting crown at forty. And he did all of this despite fighting for his country for five years, first in World War II and then in the Korean War.

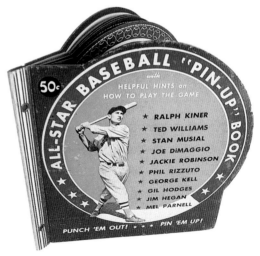

This rare All Star pin-up book had Williams on its cover and other stars inside. Fans could carefully rip the circular pictures of the players out of the book and mount them on a wall.

How to play base-ball? Who else would you turn to but Ted Williams, the Splendid Splinter?

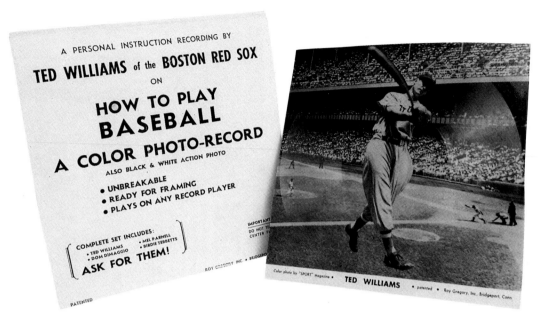

A PERSONAL INSTRUCTION RECORDING BY

TED WILLIAMS of the BOSTON RED SOX

ON

HOW TO PLAY
BASEBALL

A COLOR PHOTO-RECORD

ALSO BLACK & WHITE ACTION PHOTO

• UNBREAKABLE
• READY FOR FRAMING
• PLAYS ON ANY RECORD PLAYER

COMPLETE SET INCLUDES:
• TED WILLIAMS   • MEL PARNELL
• DOM DIMAGGIO   • BIRDIE TEBBETTS

ASK FOR THEM!

Color photo by "SPORT" magazine   TED WILLIAMS   • patented   • Roy Gregory, Inc., Bridgeport, Conn.

All of this is hard for any fan to sort out. So perhaps the easiest way to explain the Red Sox star's greatness lies in just one fact: Williams was the last man to hit .400.

Ted was such a good hitter that other players would stare at him. "Whenever we'd play Boston, I'd get right up on the edge of the dugout steps when Williams was up and I'd study him," admits New York's Mickey Mantle. "I played with Joe D. and I admired Joe D., but I have to say Ted Williams is the best hitter I ever saw. He had tremendous hand-eye coordination, good bat speed, a great turn, power, concentration. He had it all."

Fans loved Williams as well. "I think people admired him because his goal was to be the best hitter," asserts Mike Saunders, a Boston fan who has a basement full of Williams memorabilia. "He worked hard at it. Every year, he'd start out to be the best and he was. He never let up, never took it easy."

Williams himself described his ambition: "I wanted people to see me walk down a street, point to me, and say, there goes the greatest hitter who ever lived."

It didn't surprise people that he was that good, but it did surprise them that he was that good right away. He hit .323 his very first season with the Red Sox, crashing thirty-one home runs and batting in 145 runs. Looking back, that should not have been a shock.

45

TEDDY BALLGAME

I followed the Red Sox since I was a little kid. The first summer I was a fan was '41, the summer Williams hit .406. Tickets were expensive and we didn't get to any games that summer, so I listened to a lot of games on the radio. Adults can't listen to a game on the radio because you always have to go to do something, but kids can. Kids have nothin' to do but listen to the ballgame. So I listened to Ted Williams, city to city, month to month, hit .400. The funny thing was, after he did it, being a kid, I thought he'd hit .400 every year. I think he did, too.

—LENNY HEADEY, 56, of Worcester, Massachusetts

A '40s Williams button.

Two Ted Williams models of the old sticker-barrel bats, popular for thirty years. Manufacturers sold them as promotional bats with different players on stickers—Cobb, Ruth, etc.

A signed Ted Williams bat from the Cooperstown Bat Company.

Williams baseball-button box.

A contemporary Williams statue.

TED WILLIAMS

Below, a Ted Williams–Jimmy Fund tag.

What made [Williams] great was that he worked so very hard on hitting. He wanted to be the best and was. I never met anyone so determined to succeed. He loved challenges. He'd get angry when a team would put the "Williams shift" on him. Now, a normal guy would adjust and hit eighty-eight singles a year to an open left field. Not Ted. He'd take the challenge and hit right into that shift. If he had just hit the other way, which he could have all the time, I think he would have hit .400 five or six times.

—Broadcaster MEL ALLEN

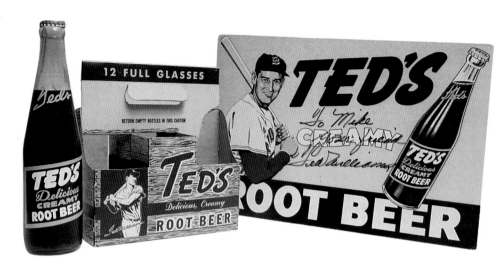

And Ted's own root beer.

Above and right, one of New England's most popular sodas advertised by one of New England's most popular ballplayers, Moxie has been downed on hot days from the Berkshires to Provincetown since the turn of the century.

Williams had first started playing ball in the second grade in San Diego, California, where he grew up, and by the fifth or sixth grade he'd become a feared presence in the playground. When teachers at his grade school let the kids play ball before school every day, Ted Williams was the first kid at the athletic office to pull out the bats and balls.

In high school Ted was a legend, hitting so many balls over the fence and onto the school roof during his first-day tryout that the custodian ordered the coach to switch fields. Everything after that blended into the legend.

After hitting .430 in high school, Williams signed with the minor-league San Diego Padres in 1936 and later played with Minneapolis's minor-league team, moving to the Red Sox system in 1937. In 1938 he hit .366 in the minors with 43 home runs. In 1939, his rookie season, he ripped apart the American League, anchoring a formidable lineup that included second baseman Bobby Doerr and slugger Jimmie Foxx. He hit righties. He hit lefties. He hit for average and he hit for power.

"I think the key to Ted's success was that he worked very hard at it," mused teammate Mel Parnell. "He had amazing natural ability, but so do lots of guys. He worked hard every day. He always took extra batting practice. He'd walk around

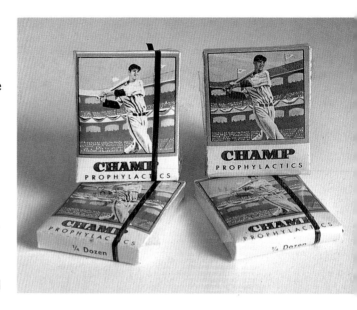

Ted's contribution to birth control.

A Williams button festooned with ribbon, bat, and ball.

Teddy Ballgame in print.

A happy Williams celebrates after another great 1941 game, the year he became the last man to hit .400. Coming into the last day of the season his average was .3995, a figure the commissioner of baseball declared could count as .400. But Williams wouldn't hear of it. Instead of sitting out the final doubleheader to protect his average, he went six for eight and raised his average to .406.

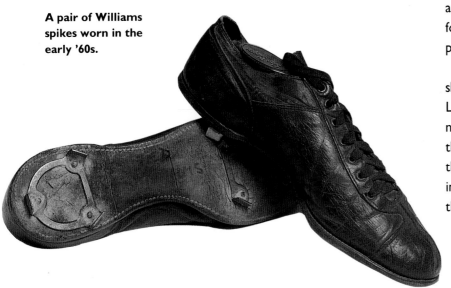

A pair of Williams spikes worn in the early '60s.

all day holding a bat, just to keep the feel right. He treated batting practice just like a game. He would get enraged at himself for grounding out to third base in batting practice. That's what made him so good."

With Williams in place, the Red Sox should have been golden. But only aging Lefty Grove pitched fifteen or more winning games and the team couldn't get near the pennant. In 1940 Yawkey strengthened the Sox further by hiring quiet, hardworking Dom DiMaggio. That year everybody in the Boston infield hit more than twenty

A Red Sox beanie and a Williams book from the Barnes All-Star Library.

TED WILLIAMS

50 Cents

THE BARNES ALL-STAR LIBRARY

BY TOM MEANY with action photos

BOSTON RED SOX

Williams has appeared on just about every baseball card and picture set out there.

home runs and Williams hit a sizzling .344. The team was a statistical marvel, unbeatable on paper. So what happened? They finished a sour fourth.

Although 1941 was another dismal year for the Sox, who finished seventeen games behind the Yankees, it was a historic year for baseball, for in this single season the two greatest feats of modern baseball history were accomplished: Joe DiMaggio hit safely in fifty-six consecutive games and Ted Williams became the last man ever to hit .400.

DiMaggio's remarkable streak and Williams's sensational season have been heavily chronicled, but the tale of Williams's last games that year still gives fans a chill. Williams got an okay from manager Joe Cronin to sit out the doubleheader on the final day of the season with a .3995 average that the commissioner of baseball had decreed would round off to .400. But hitting .3995 was not hitting .400, he insisted, and he forced Cronin into penciling him into the lineup. That overcast day in Philadelphia Williams put the exclamation point on the greatest season since Ruth hit sixty homers, as he went six for eight and finished the year at .406.

Red Sox and
Williams souvenirs
from the '40s.

1948 BOSTON RED SOX

THE BEST TEAM NEVER TO WIN A SERIES

THE LATE '40s

World War II stopped just about everything. A number of Red Sox players including Ted Williams rushed off to join the military and the team staggered through the war years. Yet when the 1946 season began, the Red Sox played like the war had never happened. The top players were back from the service and the Sox were back in their 1938 and 1939 form. They hammered everybody, winning an astonishing 104 games and claiming the pennant. One of the stars of that team was Johnny Pesky, a good fielder who became one of the American League's top shortstops. Pesky played for the Sox just one year before he left for the war, but when he returned in 1946 he became one of the league's most powerful hitters with 208 hits and a .335 batting average. Another star was Hall-of-Famer Bobby Doerr, the consistent second baseman who anchored the infield and hit .271 that year. Dom DiMaggio, Joe's brother, had another fine year, hitting .316. And of course Ted Williams returned, testy with the press and his fans but hitting .342 with 38 homers and 123 RBIs and almost winning another Triple Crown.

It was a fine year, 1946, but it was also the year the great Sox jinx began. The jinx, painfully familiar to Boston fans by now, crept into the team bats sometime in the summer of 1946 and took up permanent residence. What the legendary jinx entails is that no matter how well Boston

Johnny Pesky was a great player for the Sox in the '40s, and today, serving as assistant to general manager Lou Gorman, he remains a revered figure in Boston, as familiar around Fenway as the Citgo sign.

57

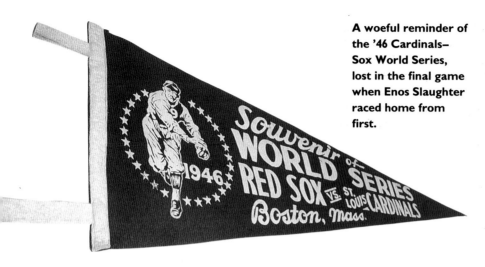

A woeful reminder of the '46 Cardinals–Sox World Series, lost in the final game when Enos Slaughter raced home from first.

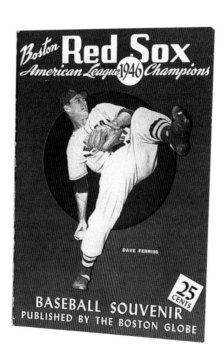

One of the many Sox books, programs, and special sections published by the *Boston Globe,* this one from 1946 featuring sensation Dave "Boo" Ferriss on the cover. He won twenty-one games as a rookie in 1945 and twenty-five in '46 before asthma cut short his career.

plays, the team never quite makes it to the World Series, or if it does, Boston loses. That's exactly what happened in 1946.

The Sox should have taken apart the Cardinals but they couldn't. They should have taken apart the American League, at least, the next year, but they could finish no better than third. That year Ted Williams started to see the "Williams shift" for the first time as managers, aware that he tended to hit to the right, overloaded that side of the field, often leaving left field completely unprotected. It didn't help. Williams just kept getting better. He hit .343 that season and won the Triple Crown for the second time, although the team couldn't quite match his pace.

The 1948 season was another one the fans thought would mean October baseball, but the jinx just grew. This time the Red Sox wound up tied for the pennant, but they lost it in a playoff. Fans were thunderstruck that fate could slay them in two of three years. They didn't have long for the lightning bolt to hit the same place three times.

Determined to win the pennant, the Red Sox played spectacular baseball in 1949, only to lose the flag to the hated Yankees on the final day of the season, 5–3. Williams at least won an MVP award and star pitcher Mel Parnell stunned every-

A ticket stub, in great condition, from the '46 World Series. This bleacher seat cost all of $1.20.

An overly optimistic entreprenuer produced these Boston Red Sox World's Champions buttons in 1946, the year the Sox lost to the Cards.

A rare, untorn ticket to the '46 World Series—a box seat for $7.20.

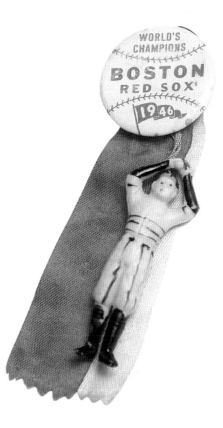

one in baseball with his stellar 25–7 season, but the jinx had learned to love Fenway. The Red Sox would not win a pennant again until 1967.

"We were never mad that we lost the Series and then barely missed two straight pennants," insisted Parnell, one of the most beloved Red Sox ever. "We were just disappointed. I don't think there's anything more heartbreaking in baseball than to come that close—just a game—and not get there. The players felt bad for the fans, too, because we had

Rudy York crosses the plate after smacking a three-run homer in the first inning of game three in the '46 World Series to put the Sox ahead for good. They won the game 4–0.

Bobby Doerr has Enos "Country" Slaughter out by a country mile in the third game of the '46 Series as Slaughter tries to break up a double play. Having forced out Slaughter, Doerr leaps above him and throws to first. Slaughter would get even in game seven by scoring from first on a single.

The three DiMaggio brothers, together at a spring training game in 1940. Vince (left) played for Cincinnati, Joe starred with the Yankees, and dapper Dom (right) was with the Red Sox.

A Boston fan cut this photo of Dom DiMaggio out of a magazine and got his signature on it. DiMaggio has to be the most underrated other-brother in baseball. While Joe was earning much glory (deserved), people forget that Dom was establishing himself as a stellar player who made the All Star team three times.

T he one regret I have is that I didn't hit .300 lifetime. [DiMaggio hit .298.] One time, Tommy Henrich caught a deep fly ball I hit that was a sacrifice that brought in the winning run. He didn't have to catch it, but he did. I met him years later and he said that all his life that bothered him because he felt that maybe that one hit would have moved me up to .300. I laughed and told him to forget about it.

—DOM DIMAGGIO, Boston Red Sox

record crowds those years. The people of Boston were behind us all the way and we always felt badly that we just couldn't get there."

And what always hurt was that when the Red Sox snatched defeat from the jaws of victory, the jaws always read *New* and *York*. They lost to Cleveland in the 1948 playoffs after losses to the Yankees during the season prevented them from taking the pennant outright. They lost to the Yankees on the final day of the 1949 season. A few decades later they would lose the 1978 pennant in another playoff to the hated Yankees. Even when the Bombers weren't beating them, New York itself seemed to menace the Sox. The greatest psychological blow Boston fans ever endured was the loss to the Mets in the 1986 World Series. Where did the Mets play? Of course, New York.

The Boston–New York rivalry grew and became one of the greatest in sports. The baseball rivalry tumbled over onto the basketball court, too, as the Celtics and Knicks became mortal enemies, but it was in baseball, year after year, that the two cities became classic combatants in a rivalry that is still as hot today as it was back in 1916 or 1956.

The players have mixed reactions about the rivalry.

A Red Sox program
and scorecard, worth
a dime in 1947.

Schedules for the
Sox and the Braves
issued at the start of
the '47 season.

Programs from the
'48 and '51 seasons.

Jersey and cap of Paul Schreiber, Red Sox coach from 1947 to 1958.

More Sox ticket stubs, from '48 and '51.

"Oh, none of us hated anybody on the Red Sox. They were good ballplayers and good guys. The strength of the rivalry was that these were always two good baseball teams. If we wanted the pennant each year, we had to beat the Red Sox. They were always in our way," said Moose Skowron, first baseman for the Yankees in the '50s who played the Red Sox over a hundred times. "We were always up for them because they were a good team, not because they were the Red Sox."

"You have the geography, too, and that's a factor," said Enos Slaughter, who played for the Yankees and who single-handedly defeated the Red Sox in the '46 Series when he scored from first for the

Cardinals on a single. "New York and Boston are very close to each other. You had an intracity rivalry with the Dodgers and Giants. There was no other American League team, so Boston was closest."

Despite decades of hostility between the fans of each team, everybody agrees that the rivalry is good for baseball.

"It's one of those great American events, like the coming of snow or the end of school," said the late Commissioner of Baseball Bart Giamatti. "Fathers pass that rivalry down to their sons. It's a great, great part of baseball and American sports. I hope the rivalry is always there and I hope the players and fans always want it to be there."

Christian Science Monitor sportswriter Ed Rumill's press pass for the 1945 season.

The Wall? Hell, the Wall never bothered me. The wall never bothered a good pitcher. You just threw down and away and made them hit to right, that's all. I'll tell you what bothered me—the complete lack of foul territory. A popup was in the seats. If we played in Yankee Stadium, with all that foul territory, we'd have won a lot more games. We'd have shut down a lot of power hitters who are always popping stuff away.

—MEL PARNELL, Boston Red Sox

The Monster was all psychological, all in the head.

—JOE DIMAGGIO, New York Yankees

THE GREEN MONSTER

Tony C. [Conigliaro] hit a rocket off me that was probably the hardest ball ever hit off me, much harder than anything I remember. It was rising, almost like it was picking up speed, when it smashed into the Wall about two feet from the top. There was this crash, like a car accident, and then the ball dropped straight down. We held him to a single. If that wall wasn't there, I swear that ball would have gone over five hundred feet.

—RALPH TERRY, New York Yankees

A piece of the old Green Monster signed by Yaz, flanked by a Moxie sign with Ted Root Beer bottle caps.

I think the Wall is the great equalizer. Sure, you lose some home runs over it, but there's a lot of guys, Al Kaline and Mantle come to mind, who'd rap shots off the Wall that wound up as singles that might have been doubles or triples somewhere else. It balances out.

—DICK RADATZ, ace Red Sox reliever

That left field wall was so close that if you were a righthanded pitcher and threw sidearm, your knuckles would scrape it.

—LEFTY GOMEZ, New York Yankees

THE UNFABULOUS FIFTIES

1950–1960

The 1950s were a quiet and peaceful time for America. World War II receded into memory and drive-in movies began to appear. Convertibles roared down California highways. Eddie Fisher got married a lot. The Rockefellers got richer. The Commons got greener. The Berkshires got prettier. The Kennedys took over quietly in Massachusetts. Cape Cod developed into Boston's favorite vacation spot, and Lucy ruled television airwaves.

Out at Fenway Park, the '50s were even slower and quieter. Three factors transformed the Sox into the Rip van Winkles of the diamond and helped put fans to sleep for the decade as well. The first was bad luck. Bobby Doerr's career was cut short in 1951 when his bad back caught up with him. Then Ted Williams went back into the service to fight in the Korean War. And Harry Agganis died. The second problem, not unconnected to the first, was that the lineup of the early decade changed fast. Doerr retired. Williams wasn't available. Jimmy Piersall had a mental breakdown. Johnny Pesky and Walt Dropo were traded to Detroit, and Mickey McDermott was traded to Washington. The third blow to the Sox was that the Yankees bloomed in the Fifties. The New York powerhouse, with Mickey Mantle, Roger Maris, and company, dominated baseball and especially dominated the American League. They won every pennant in

The four balls pitcher Mel Parnell holds represent the 4–0 score in his 1953 no-hitter against the hated Yankees. Parnell, one of the most consistent pitchers in all of baseball, won 123 and lost 75.

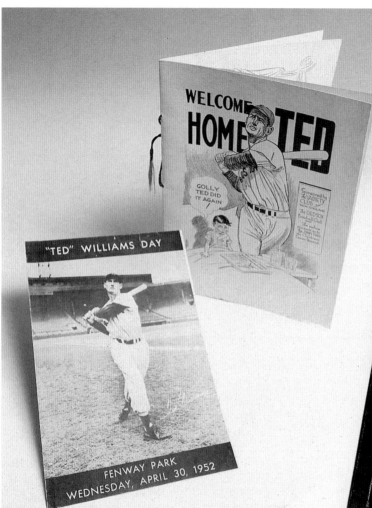

Souvenir programs from **Ted Williams Day, April 30, 1952,** held to celebrate Williams's return from a military stint. Between his service in World War II and the Korean War, Ted lost five years of his career to the military, but still managed to shatter records of every ilk.

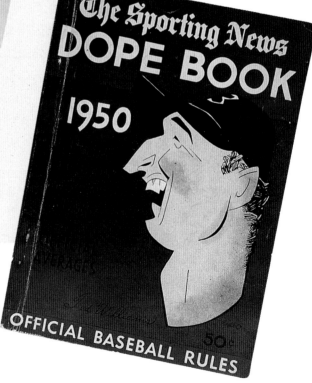

The annual *Sporting News Dope Book* was no dope—here's Teddy Ballgame on the cover in 1950.

the decade except those in '54 and '59. No matter how well the Red Sox might have played, they would never have outplayed the Yankees.

The players Boston did have in the '50s brought fans some wonderful memories though, and while the Sox never really threatened, they claimed respectable third place finishes in '50, '51, '57 and '58, and finished fourth in '53, '54, '55, and '56.

If the standings weren't so stellar, certainly the players were memorable. Piersall was a hyperactive, flamboyant

Buttons of the wildly eccentric Jimmy Piersall and the dependable infielder Frank Malzone.

Jersey and hat belonging to Ted Williams.

Away jersey belonging to a Red Sox coach.

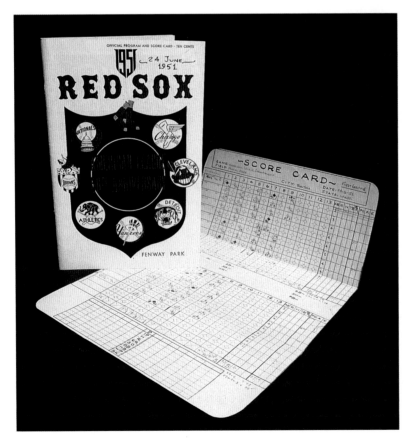

This is an autographed Jackie Jensen bat, signed by one of the Sox's more promising players but one whose fear of flying helped force him to retire early.

player (and a good one) who just couldn't resist taunting and teasing the opposition. He once pretended he was a pig while leading off first base and so rattled old Satchel Paige that Paige loaded the bases and gave up a grand slam home run to Sammy White. Later Piersall checked himself into a sanitarium where he was diagnosed as having mental problems. He was out for a season and when he returned he was far more subdued, but now and again he reverted to character. His most publicized stunt came much later, in 1963, when he hit his hundredth home run while playing for the Mets. As soon as he knew it was gone, he raced around the bases—backwards. Piersall's story, and his pain, were chronicled in the book and movie *Fear Strikes Out.*

   The 1954 season saw the arrival of the legendary Jackie Jensen, the first genuine two-sport All-American to hit the majors since Jackie Robinson. Like Robinson, Jensen was an All-American running

This fancy 1951 program celebrating the fiftieth anniversary of the American League contrasts nicely with the triple-folded scorecard next to it from early in the century.

Above, a Red Sox
bank from the '50s.

Below, this twelve-inch-high Red Sox ceramic does nothing but stand on a shelf. So why did Red Sox diehard collector Rick Sachs buy it? "It said Red Sox, didn't it?" he explained.

back (at the University of Southern California) and a great baseball player. He became a star right away, hitting 100 RBIs in five different seasons. In 1958 he was voted MVP in the American League. But in 1960 Jensen announced that he was leaving baseball forever, the result of his bone-rattling fear of flying. He did come back for one more season, a mediocre one, but in 1961 he left for good—by train.

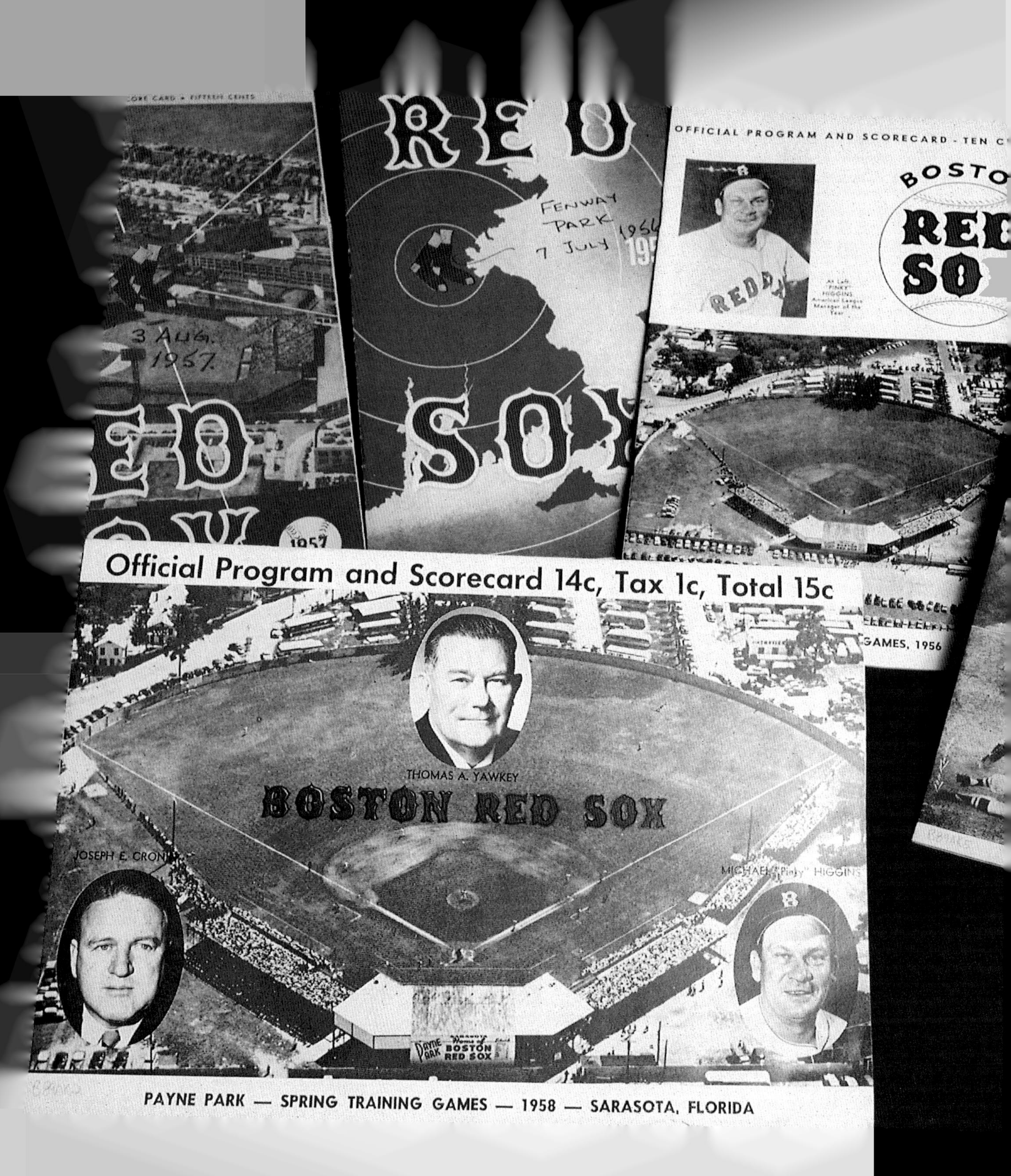

SCORE CARD • FIFTEEN CENTS

3 AUG. 1957

RED SOX

1957

RED SOX

Fenway Park 7 July 1956

OFFICIAL PROGRAM AND SCORECARD - TEN C

At left, "PINKY" HIGGINS American League Manager of the Year.

BOSTO

RED SO

GAMES, 1956

Official Program and Scorecard 14c, Tax 1c, Total 15c

THOMAS A. YAWKEY

BOSTON RED SOX

JOSEPH E. CRONIN

MICHAEL "Pinky" HIGGINS

BOSTON RED SOX

PAYNE PARK — SPRING TRAINING GAMES — 1958 — SARASOTA, FLORIDA

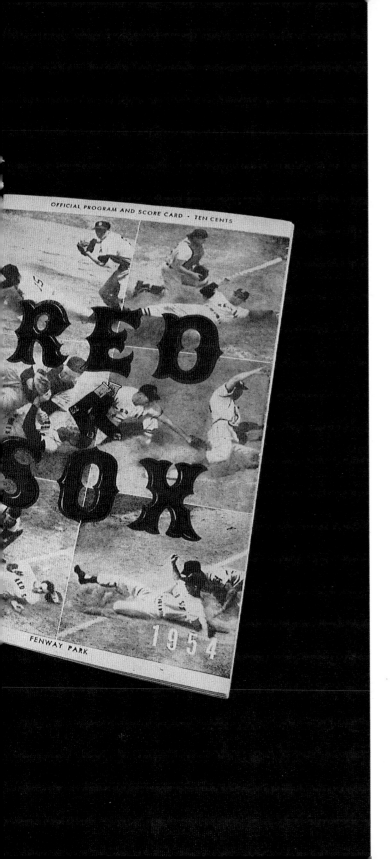

A Sarasota training
camp guide to the
Sox and the annual
press guide of 1961.

This group of pro-
grams from the
1950s has stood the
test of time as well
as life in a collector's
closet.

Shadows on Fenway on a June afternoon.

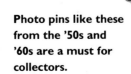

Photo pins like these from the '50s and '60s are a must for collectors.

Then there was the sad story of the sensational Harry Agganis, another All-American in two sports like Jensen. Agganis, a quarterback for Boston University, joined the Sox in 1954 and hit .251. He returned in '55 and was hitting .313 when a case of pneumonia put him into the hospital in May. Soon after he returned to the team he was brought down by fevers and chest pains and was hospitalized again. On June 27, Agganis died of a blood clot.

Another two-sport star for Boston in that era was Gene Conley. In the mid-'50s he had flowered as a pitcher with Milwaukee and later moved to the Sox, winning fifteen games in 1962. But the amazing thing about Conley was that he played two sports without leaving home—the 6'9" athlete was a forward for the Boston Celtics in the winter and a pitcher for the Red Sox in summer.

Boston's first black player, Pumpsie Green, wasn't signed until late in the decade, in 1959, a delay that angered many fans who had watched every other team in major-league baseball integrate years before. (Ironically, back in the late '40s Boston turned down a chance to sign Jackie Robinson.) Green hit .246 during his brief career with the Sox.

A steady and popular infield developed in the '50s. Frank Malzone, a product

Schedules from the '50s, including two pocket-sized versions.

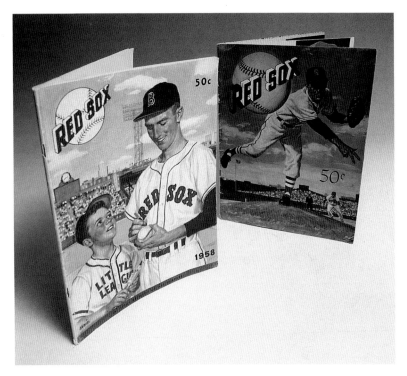

The gorgeous illustrations on the covers of these Red Sox programs captured the spirit of the '50s.

of the team's farm system, became one of the best third basemen in the American League, joined in the infield by Pete Runnels. Williams, of course, played left field, and at the end of the decade the Red Sox signed Vic Wertz, who drove in 103 runs in 1960.

"It was a wonderful time to be a kid and follow the team," said longtime fan Rick Sachs of Worcester, Massachusetts. "We didn't win any pennants, but we had some great teams and terrific players. They were the kind of guys who'd sign autographs, talk to kids, chat with you. They made it such a pleasure going to the ballpark."

In a way, you know the Red Sox will break your heart in the end, but you love them anyway. That's what being a fan is all about, isn't it?

—TOM GILMARTIN, Fenway usher
for twenty-nine years

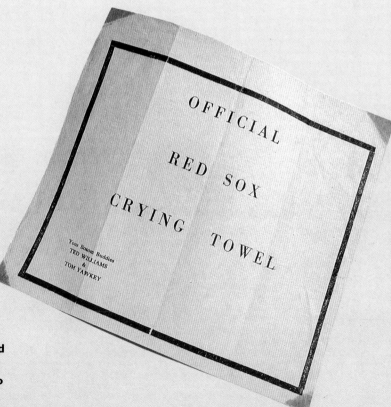

A Fenway banner,
above, with one of
the many official Red
Sox crying towels,
this one dedicated to
Ted Williams and
Tom Yawkey.

GOING AND COMING
1960–1978

The first year of the 1960s was the last year in the career of Ted Williams. He closed the book on baseball at the age of forty-two and did it in sparkling style with a .316 season, twenty-nine home runs, and a home run in his very last at-bat. The combative Williams, who had a strained relationship with writers and fans most of his career, refused to tip his cap to the fans as he rounded the bases after he hit his final home run. "I just couldn't do it," he said. "It just would not have been me."

Miraculously, the spring after Williams vacated left field, a talented young player named Carl Yastrzemski occupied it. The slugging outfielder out of Long Island and Notre Dame came to Boston after two great years in the minors. He hit .266 in his first year, disappointing fans who, of course, hoped he would turn out to be the next Williams. Yaz did better in 1962, hitting .296, and he won the American League batting championship in 1963 with .321.

The team was awful in the early '60s, however, and Yaz's heroics did little good. They did him little good, either. "I was never satisfied with myself in those first few years," he said later, after election to baseball's Hall of Fame. "My rookie year was very difficult. I put a lot of pressure on myself. I was playing left field where Williams played and there was that

Yastrzemski where he belonged—at bat.

In his very last at-bat in his very last game, Teddy Ballgame hit a home run, his 521st. Here he crosses home plate, greeted by catcher Jim Pagli-aroni. The next year, 1961, Yaz came up to take his place.

pressure, too. Even those years when I'd hit .320 or more I didn't feel like I was contributing, that I was good enough. I'd go two for four and feel bad about the two times I didn't get on base. It affected me at the ballpark and at home. I just was never satisfied."

Eventually Yastrzemski's perfection-ism began to sink into the rest of the team,

ON THE AIR

SPECIAL RED SOX BASEBALL EDITION
from
NEW ENGLAND'S BIG LEAGUE STATIONS!

THE BOSTON GLOBE

BASEBALL SPRING TRAINING CAMP

Saturday, May 2, 1964
Fenway Park
Boston, Mass.

BILL MONBOUQUETTE
MEDFORD H. S.—1953

Left, a loyal Red Sox dog on his way to spring training camp, and above, Radio Red Sox with Curt Gowdy.

and suddenly in 1967 the Sox made their move. Their successes that season took everyone by surprise. "I think, looking back, that everybody in the country except the players thought the '67 pennant was a miracle," mused pitcher Darrell Brandon, a rookie back in 1966. "We felt strongly that we could do it back in September of '66. We were playing very well in the last quarter of '66 and started out well in '67. We thought we had a shot the whole season long."

Nobody else did. After all, even with hard-hitting new superstar Carl Yastrzemski, hadn't the lowly Red Sox struggled in ninth the previous year? The team batting average was only .251, every pitcher had a losing record, and the manager, Dick Williams, was a rookie pilot.

Yaz

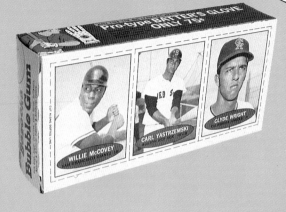

I played with Yaz and appreciated him, sure, but I also played against him when I was with the Phillies. That's when I found out how truly great he was. I couldn't touch him as a pitcher, just couldn't touch him. He wouldn't swing at bad pitches. Could never get him on a high one. He had a good eye; would walk a lot. He could hit anybody's fastball, and I mean anybody. If you can't blow them by a guy, you just can't consistently get him out. That was Yaz's great strength. People just couldn't get him out. He'd walk, he'd single, he'd homer, he'd sacrifice for you—he'd be there.

—DARRELL BRANDON
Pitcher on the 1967 Sox Wonder Team

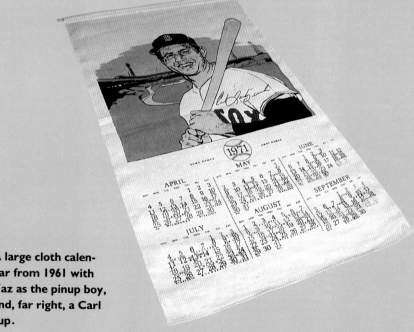

A large cloth calendar from 1961 with Yaz as the pinup boy, and, far right, a Carl cup.

Carl was a multi-faceted player. He was always a good, consistent hitter. You always worried about him because he could hit a quickie single if they needed it and he could hit one out. Just having him at the plate gave them an edge.

—JOHNNY BENCH, Cincinnati Reds

Yaz's greatness was in his consistency. He'd always hurt you. Early innings, late innings, extra innings. He could hit anybody and hit it anywhere. Lots of guys were streak players. Not Yaz. He was always good. Always.

—MICKEY MANTLE, New York Yankees

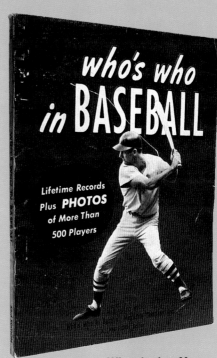

Who else but Yastrzemski would be on the '68 cover of *Who's Who in Baseball* after his titanic '67 season (forty-four home runs, 121 RBIs, .326 average).

But the Red Sox stayed in the race all the way, behind the ferocious pitching of Jim Lonborg (22–9) and the unbelievable hitting of Yastrzemski, who won the Triple Crown (the last person to do it) with forty-four home runs, 121 RBIs, and a .326 average. Yaz was consistent from the start of the season to the end, posting unbelievable numbers every week and every month of the summer and on into September. Many say that this was the single greatest season an individual player ever had.

"We had a good lineup and good pitching, but, really, it was Yaz," said catcher Russ Gibson, a rookie that year. "Those Triple Crown numbers of his are awesome, but they don't tell half the story. There'd be two on and Yaz would homer. The game would be tied in extra innings and we'd have a guy on second and Yaz

The way it worked out was this: the very first game I played as a Red Sox player was against the Yankees in Yankee Stadium. Is that heady? In that game, I went two for four off Whitey Ford. Our pitcher, Bill Rohr, threw a no-hitter into the ninth inning, with me catching him all the way. The second game, the next day, was at Yankee Stadium and it went eighteen innings— eighteen!—and I caught it the whole way. That second night, when I went to sleep, I said to myself, 'Jesus, playing for the Boston Red Sox is going to be fun.'

—RUSS GIBSON, Boston Red Sox

Left, red, white, and blue press guides for the Red Sox.

Above, a ticket to the '61 All Star game held at Fenway.

Souvenirs of the '60s.

Left, a few of the sillier Sox mementoes from the '60s: two straw hats, one signed by Yaz from the '67 series, the other with a Yaz button, guarded by a Red Sox stuffed doll.

would drive him in with a double off the wall. He was the greatest clutch hitter I ever saw. It was like he was waiting all afternoon just so he could get up and win the game for you."

It wasn't easy, though. A few gentlemen on the Minnesota Twins, the Chicago White Sox, and the Detroit Tigers seemed to feel the stretch heroism might suit them just as well as the upstarts from the Boston Common. But the Sox stayed hot that summer. They were 19–10 in July, 20–15 in August, and then, during the first three weeks of September, 15–11. As the four teams raced down to the wire, less than two games separating them in the standings, Boston got tough. Yaz led them with twenty-three hits in his last forty-four at-bats in the pennant stretch, ten in his last thirteen at-bats, seven in his last eight, and four for four on the last day of the season. Jim Lonborg was steady and sharp on the mound and reliever John Wyatt, with plenty of pressure on all summer, pulled off twenty saves.

As football weather started to set in gently across all of New England, the White Sox faded away, their .225-hitting club unable to generate much power. In the last two games of the season the Twins met the Red Sox and Boston triumphed in both games—but thanks to Detroit the pennant remained just out of reach.

Dick "Monster" Radatz, the first superstar relief pitcher with 122 saves. "Today, you have nothing but relief pitching," observed Radatz.

"You've got long relief, short relief, and what they call a 'closer,' whatever that is. Hell, pretty soon you'll have relief pitchers for the second inning."

Sportsmanship Club

OFFICIAL RULES

Always play hard, but play fair.

Be good to your body, it's the only way to live.

Regular, daily exercise makes sense . . . and athletes.

Recognize what you are and what you are not; then develop what talent you have.

Never let up, always bear down.

Eat plenty of protein foods—meat, vegetables and bread with extra protein.

Only a few can reach stardom . . . but all of us can try.

Appreciate the efforts of your teammates.

Learning in school now, means earning a good living later on.

Don't forget, the name of any game is FUN.

Defeat can help . . . if you learn from it.

Success in sports-and in life-is spelled "hard work".

ARNOLD

Arnold Bread Sportsmanship Club's Official Rules, as propounded by club president Yastrzemski, including such gems of wisdom as "Success in sports—and in life—is spelled 'hard work' ". Below, a photo cut-out of Yaz.

It wasn't important that Yaz won the Triple Crown. What was so important, and made him so valuable, is that he'd get that clutch hit every single time he was up. You'd have to check the score sheets, but I doubt he didn't get a hit when we had a guy on. He was unreal. I watched a lot of baseball as a kid on TV and since, in twenty-four years, I've watched a lot more and I'll tell you . . . nobody ever had a season like Yaz in '67. Nobody.

—RUSS GIBSON, Boston Red Sox

89

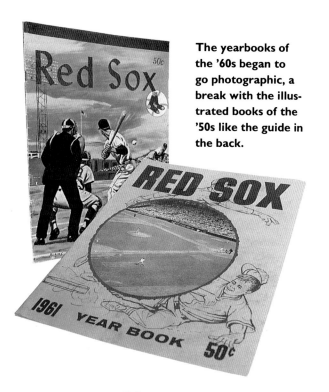

The yearbooks of the '60s began to go photographic, a break with the illustrated books of the '50s like the guide in the back.

Foldout newspaper poster of the team in the '60s.

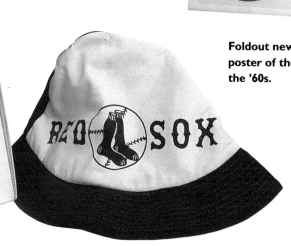

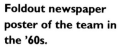

What would a summer day on the Cape be without a Red Sox cap? On the left is another necessity (?), a plastic Red Sox doll.

Yaz clouts a fourth-inning home run in the second game of the '67 Series off Cardinal pitcher Dick Hughes. Catcher Tim McCarver, now a broadcaster, is behind the plate.

The scoreboard on the Green Monster tells the story as Jim Lonborg throws the last pitch of the second game in the '67 Series. Curt Flood popped out on the pitch to give the Sox a 5–0 win.

Reggie Smith slides in front of Tim McCarver's tag to put the Sox ahead 3–1 in game five of the '67 Series.

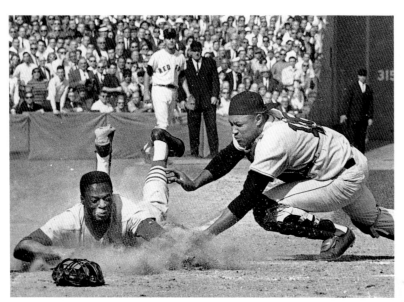

Left, ouch! Fleet-footed Cardinal Lou Brock, until 1991 the leading base stealer of all time, slides safely into home, beating Elston Howard's tag in the '67 World Series. He had hot-footed it to the plate from second base on Curt Flood's single.

Above, renowned for his bat, left fielder Carl Yastrzemski makes a leaping grab of Curt Flood's shot to left in the second game of the '67 Series. He made this extraordinary catch even after moving in too fast and misjudging the ball, but he turned quickly, chased it, and lunged.

A photographer crouching in the stands behind home plate snapped this vivid fish-eye shot of Fenway during the 1967 World Series.

The late Tony Conigliaro, one of the most beloved athletes ever to grace the playing fields of New England and a ballplayer every woman in New England had a crush on.

A button depicting Tony Conigliaro, Boston's beloved but tragic hero.

TONY CONIGLIARO
BOSTON RED SOX

94

The '67 World Series tickets were among the strangest ever, with maps of the world on them (get it?).

Although the Sox looked to be solidly on top, Detroit could force a playoff game if it won a doubleheader against the Angels that same day. The Tigers took the first game, but late in the afternoon of that final, dramatic day they fell to California. Throughout New England bells rang and horns honked as the Miracle Sox won the pennant.

But as strong as they were, with all their momentum, and with great fans behind them, once again the jinxed Sox just couldn't make it to the top of the mountain. Fighting tooth and nail, they lost the World Series in seven games to the Saint Louis Cardinals and red-hot Bob Gibson. "They just kept coming and coming," Gibson remembered with respect. "They wouldn't let up, not for an inning, not for a minute. Thank God the Series wasn't an eight-game affair."

Despite the Series loss, the Sox were on cloud nine. "It was a great thrill to win that pennant, even though we didn't win the World Series," said Yastrzemski. "It wasn't just winning it for ourselves. It was winning it for everybody, all the people in New England and all the Americans out there who rooted for the underdogs from Boston. It was a terrific feeling to do that."

Newspaper specials on the pennant winners from '67 and '46.

A 1967 American League championship ring.

A trio of press guides, including a '68 guide that bally-hoos the '67 pennant winners.

Included in this display of memorabilia are old ink pens shaped like bats, pennants, and a rare button featuring Tony and Billy Conigliaro. Tony, of course, was one of the Sox's great heroes, but his brother Billy also played for the team from 1969 to 1971.

Two buttons from the '75 Series, one of the greatest sporting events of all time in which the Red Sox and the Cincinnati Reds battled to a virtual standstill—finally broken by the Reds.

Bad luck returned the next year, however, with the remarkable Lonborg disabled all season after a skiing accident. The team slumped to fourth in 1968, third in '69, third in '70, and fizzled for years. Then came another chance at glory in '75 with a powerhouse lineup of Yaz, Rico Petrocelli, Dwight Evans, Tony Conigliaro (back for twenty-one games as a designated hitter), Carlton Fisk, and two sensational rookies—Fred Lynn and Jim Rice. The team's pitching was also solid, featuring Rick Wise, Luis Tiant, and Bill Lee.

That year Boston fell through a hole in the ground and emerged into the sunlight of perhaps the greatest World Series of all time, this against the powerful Big Red Machine of Cincinnati with Tony Perez, Pete Rose, Johnny Bench, and Joe Morgan. The two clubs battled each other game for game, inning for inning, out for

out, until the sixth game, which many folks who were there insist was the single most dramatic Series game of all time.

Both teams mobilized their best pitching and their best hitting, but neither could dent the other's armor. With what seemed like all of Boston (and Cape Cod, too) jammed into old Fenway, the drama and the tension built to a fever pitch. The score was tied 6–6 as the twelfth inning began. Boston's Fisk hit a deep, deep shot toward the left-field fence, but, like every

This '75 World Series button hails the Sox as the "Peace Party." Maybe a little too peaceful, since they lost the Series in seven games.

other event in Red Sox history since 1918, it seemed to be going foul. Fisk stood at the plate and waved it fair and willed it fair and finally it hit the pole for a home run. No one in Fenway leaped as high as Fisk when the ball went out.

Unfortunately there was still a seventh game to be played, at which point the jinx choked the Series out of the Red Sox. In one of the closest games in Series history, Cincinnati broke a 3–3 tie in the ninth to win the game and the Series.

"That was the most exciting Series I ever played in and, since I was a kid, ever saw," said Johnny Bench, the Red's catcher in the games. "Fenway is an intimate park, and nothing you saw on television could compare to the tension in that park when Fisk hit that homer in game six. That was unreal. I'm glad we won it, but everybody in Boston should be proud of that Series. It was a great one. Nobody really lost it."

Carlton Fisk urging his historic twelfth-inning home run to stay fair. It did, and its cooperation won game six of the 1975 World Series for the Sox.

Sox ash tray.

Fisk and half of Boston went delirious as he crossed home plate after the famous game six home run.

I was standing in the walkway near the box seats behind the Red Sox dugout when Fisk hit that home run in the sixth game of the '75 Series. I was swaying and pushing my body just like he was to somehow make it stay fair. And it did! The woman sitting in front of me jumped up, turned around, and kissed me!

—TOM GILMARTIN, Fenway usher for twenty-nine years

99

Left, photo decal glasses saw their heyday in the early '70s, these depicting Carlton Fisk, Fred Lynn, and Bill Lee.

Opposite, Yaz at bat against the Yankees, smacking hit number 3,000.

The Red Sox finished third in '76, the year old Tom Yawkey finally died, second in '77, and roared out of the starting gate in 1978 with perhaps the best team in baseball. The Sox were 23–7 in May, 18–7 in June, and by July 19 they had established an uncatchable ten-game lead on the Milwaukee Brewers along with a fourteen-game lead on the Yankees. The only question was by how many games the Red Sox would take the division . . . ten? twenty?

No one is sure how it all started to unravel. The jinx, sunning on Cape Cod most of the summer, returned, and the Sox began to stumble in late July. By late August they were bleeding all over the American League. Between August 30 and September 16, Boston lost fourteen of seventeen and then another four in a row to the Yankees by the amazing scores of 15–3, 13–1, 7–0, and 7–4. The Yankees, reveling in the collapse of their rival, staged one of the most memorable drives in baseball, winning fifty-two of their last seventy-three games and tying Boston for first place. Another historic playoff game was called.

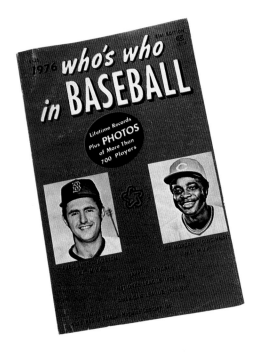

Right, rookie sensation Fred Lynn adorned the cover of many magazines following his sensational 1975 debut season, in which he hit .331 and led the American League in runs and doubles. That year he became the only man ever voted both Rookie of the Year and MVP. Lynn asked to be traded in 1981, however, in order to play in his native California; he never hit .300 again.

It's too painful to recall, but the facts are burned into everyone's memory. The Red Sox took a 2–0 lead into the seventh inning and two Yankees reached base before Bucky Dent, a lackluster .240 hitter with just four home runs all year, stepped into the box. He wafted a high, easy fly ball out toward left field, a fly ball that Yaz would be bound to grab. But the wind carried it farther and farther, out to the Green Monster and suddenly, sadly, over the wall.

The Sox never recovered. The Yankees won the playoff 5–4 after Yaz popped out with a man on third, ending the game and yet another chance at the brass ring.

"It was an unusual game," said Ron Guidry, the Yankee starter. "Bucky hit that ball and no one was at all concerned about it. Anywhere else, that would be the third out. The wind took it over, though. We were just amazed."

So was all of New England.

The rather serene pennant directly above commemorates the very turbulent '86 World Series in which the New York Mets defeated Boston in a heartstopping game. The banner on top celebrates the American bicentennial in 1976.

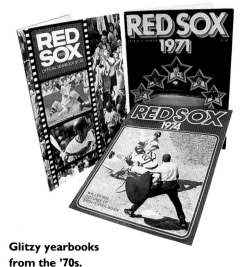

Glitzy yearbooks from the '70s.

Abe Lincoln's picture never made it on this fiver, but then how many home runs did Honest Abe ever hit?

Dwight Evans round-
ing third on a home
run early in his
career. The amiable
"Dewey" played at
Fenway fifteen sea-
sons. Fans were
stunned when he was
traded.

NO RETREAT, NO SURRENDER

THE '80s INTO THE '90s

With the first strong swing of rookie Wade Boggs's bat in the summer of 1982, the modern Red Sox era began. Boggs's first hit, one of more than fifteen hundred so far, introduced a whole new generation of Red Sox players and Red Sox fans. The hard-hitting third baseman was soon joined by a promising young pitching prospect named Roger Clemens, now a two-time Cy Young award winner, along with Tony Armas, Marty Barrett, Rich Gedman, Mike Greenwell, Bruce Hurst, and veterans Jim Rice, Dave Henderson, and Dwight Evans (Yastrzemski retired in 1983). A whole new Red Sox team, a team for the '80s, was taking the field and winning.

That year, 1982, the Sox finished third in the Eastern Division. They slipped to sixth in 1983, but climbed back to fourth the next. In 1985 they played .500 ball and finished fifth. Then the dream year began—the dream year with the nightmare ending.

The Red Sox did everything right in 1986. Wade Boggs hit a sensational .357, and the whole lineup was full of singles, doubles, and triples. Roger Clemens gave all of baseball a day to remember in April when he struck out twenty batters in one game to set a new record. Manager John McNamara held the reins lightly, adroitly using relievers Calvin Schiraldi and Bob Stanley, getting the most out of his hitters, and providing stable

Roger Clemens, perhaps the very best pitcher in baseball. The strong right-handed hurler has won two Cy Young awards already and seems destined for Cooperstown.

105

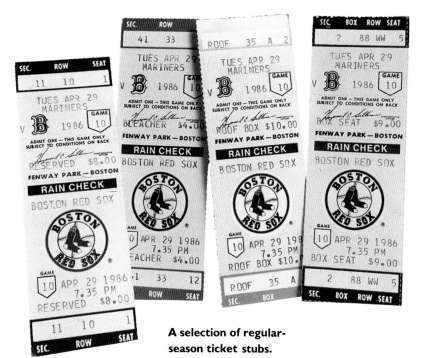

A selection of regular-season ticket stubs.

leadership in and out of the dugout. Over two million fans jammed Fenway that summer to watch the Red Sox cook. Shortly after the All-Star break, however, the team went into a dismal slump and fans shrugged. Here we go again, they said, both hands firmly around their necks in the choke hold.

Nobody heard them at Fenway. The team rebounded sharply, put together a winning streak in the middle of August, and kept the pressure up on every other team in the division, especially the Yankees. They breezed to a 5½-game lead, held it, and then won their first pennant in eleven years in a seven-game series with the Angels. California had been ahead

Ticket stubs from the ill-fated 1986 World Series, a bit more expensive by then ($40 box) than they were in '46, when box seats could be had for $7.20.

Jim Rice, another in a long line of great left fielders including Williams, Yaz, and Greenwell. Here he patrols the turf in front of the longest hand-run scoreboard in America at the base of the Green Monster.

I didn't see a ballgame till I was forty years old. A friend took me to Fenway to see my first game and I fell head over heels in love with the old place. I come back thirty to thirty-five games a season now.

—BOB COTE, 52, of Worcester, Massachusetts

I've seen it on TV a lot, but to come here. . . . Wow! It sure is big, isn't it?

—LARRY CYR, 11, on his very first visit to Fenway

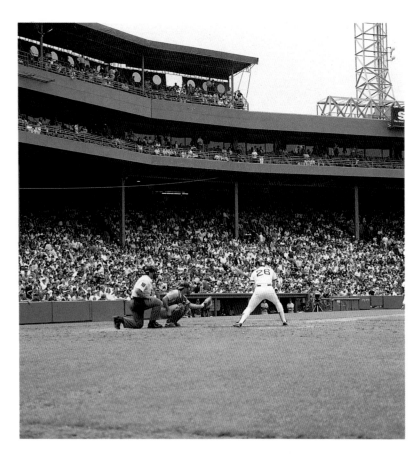

Wade Boggs at the
plate.

Batting whiz Mike
Greenwell, whose
discipline and deter-
mination have made
him a consistent .300
hitter and the latest
member of the pan-
theon of great Red
Sox hitters going
back to Ted Williams
and Tris Speaker.

 want to get big and hit just like Wade Boggs.

—GREGG SCARLATA, 7, of Easton, Massachusetts

On one of the baseballs is written:

4-29-86
20-K's
Roger
Clemens

cy young

Among a line of signed balls is one autographed by Roger Clemens on April 29, 1986, the night he fanned twenty batters for the all-time record.

three games to one going into game five, but Boston's Dave Henderson saved the team with a dramatic eleventh-inning home run and the Sox went on to take the next two games and the pennant.

The pitching staff was sharp, the hitters were on a streak, the club was hot, and everybody knew it. In the opening game of the World Series in New York, the Sox beat the New York Mets, 1–0, behind the four-hit pitching of Hurst. They completely sandbagged the Mets in game two with an eighteen-hit explosion and added a 9–3 win.

The Sox returned to Fenway and a frenzied mob. This was it. They had a two-game lead and all of New England smelled the first world championship since 1918. In game three the Mets' Lenny Dykstra led

off with a home run that broke every heart in Boston, and New York went on to win the game 7–1. The Mets than took game four behind the four-hit pitching of Ron Darling and two home runs by Gary Carter to even the series. But the Sox staggered back to win game five with a twelve-hit attack along with good pitching by Hurst.

All of this was only a prelude to the incredible last inning of game six, a game that will live in New England hearts and baseball history forever. The score was tied at the end of nine innings, but Henderson's homer and an insurance run gave Boston a 5–3 lead going into the bottom of the tenth. The Mets were down to their last out with two men on base. A wild pitch tied the game and then that infamous

ground ball somehow rolled through Bill Buckner's legs at first. The Mets won the game and all of Boston cringed.

After the heart-attack ending of game six, game seven was anticlimactic. Boston led 3–0 at one point, but it was all Mets from then on, and the New Yorkers won their second world championship, 8–5. The Sox left New York, their personal symbol of generational woe, in a hurry.

That infamous night would have been enough to crush another team, but the Red Sox survived and prevailed. After slipping to fifth in 1987, they stormed back to win the American League East again in 1988, staging a remarkable mid-season comeback behind brand-new manager Joe Morgan. Only the powerful Oakland A's were able to deprive them of the pennant, although the next year they dropped back to third. In 1990 the Sox looked tremendous all summer, but then the jinx moved in and they blew a 6½-game lead. Unwilling to be crushed, they fought back and won the division title on the very last day of the season with a sensational diving catch in the right field corner by Tom Brunansky. Boston was overwhelmed by the mighty A's again in the playoffs, inspiring critics to suggest that the Red Sox just couldn't take World Series pressure and just couldn't get that jinx off their backs. In 1990 the jinx even took on such a hal-

One of the quirkiest pitchers in Red Sox history was the enigmatic Dennis "Oil Can" Boyd. Boyd would pump his arms on strikeouts, point at players, and walk in circles around the mound. When a game in Cleveland was once called on account of fog off Lake Erie, he quipped, "That's what you get when you build a stadium on the ocean." Boyd was eventually traded.

lowed status that it became the subject of its very own book, *The Curse of the Bambino.*

But optimists point out that the Sox have won three of five divisional titles from 1986 to 1990, an impressive achievement by any standard. Optimists see a strong club unencumbered by the failures of the past.

The team is still in transition, but it has developed into a consistent threat in the American League East and it's getting stronger. Not only do the Sox have veteran stars like Greenwell, Clemens, Boggs, Brunansky, Ellis Burks, and Tony Pena, but

they have tough newcomers in Mo Vaugh, Greg Harris, Dana Kiecker, Jody Reed, Carlos Quintana, and Tom Bolton. The club has a seasoned veteran in reliever Jeff Reardon and solid starters in Joe Hesketh and Matt Young, forming a tested, competent pitching staff that no longer relies solely on Clemens. In addition to solid hitting, the team has its superstars. Wade Boggs is the best hitter in baseball, year after year, and could finish his career with a higher batting average than Ted Williams. Roger Clemens is the best pitcher in baseball. The Red Sox, along with the Dodgers, Pirates, A's, and Reds, are among the most consistent and talented teams in baseball.

Over the years, team management has always been optimistic about the future. "If you study the history of baseball, you'll notice that the teams that do well are those teams that have a balanced attack and good defensive players," mused

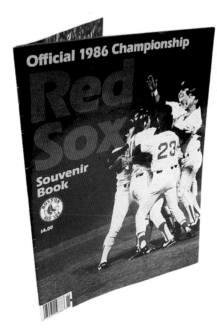

The official book on the splendid 1986 pennant.

RED SOX FANS

Check out the formal wear of the typical fan in 1915, here chatting with players.

This little trinket honors the men whose jersey numbers have been retired at Fenway— Bobby Doerr, #1; Carl Yastrzemski, #8; Ted Williams, #9; and Joe Cronin, #4.

On weekends, just about all of my business is fathers buying souvenirs for their kids and telling them stories about how it was when they'd come to Fenway with their own fathers. You often see a grandfather, father, and son coming together, with the blue-and-red Sox hats on, telling baseball stories . . . always telling baseball stories.

—MARC TALBOT, 22, souvenir salesman
from Braintree, Massachusetts

The fans in Boston were, and are, the most knowledgeable in America. They know baseball. They get down on you when you're not playing well, but they are the best fans in the world when you are doing good, or when you're up against it and need some support from the stands.

—CARL YASTRZEMSKI, Boston Red Sox

I left Boston and did not come back for twenty years. I moved back in 1984 and the fans here treated me like I was away fishing for the weekend. That's all. . . . It's like, like coming back when you're through playing and being made part of a club of some kind—where everybody's always glad to see you.

—DICK RADATZ, Boston Red Sox

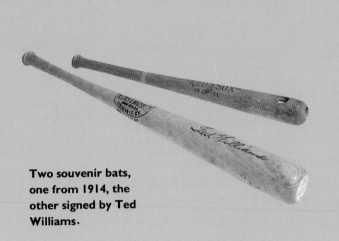

Two souvenir bats, one from 1914, the other signed by Ted Williams.

Three Red Sox bob-bin' head dolls from the '50s. The old dolls, hot collectors items today, were sold as team dolls, although some repre-sented individual players.

People say they've loved the Red Sox all their lives and will love them until the day they die. That's not a true fan. The true fan, like me, will love the Sox long after they're in the grave.

—MARGUERITE BRENNAN, 65,
OF WARWICK, RHODE ISLAND

I started watching the Red Sox on television. I fell away over the years, but now my son is seven and I'm a fan again. I take him to Fenway with me now and it's nice . . . being there with him . . . and the Red Sox.

—DON SCARLATA, 35, of Easton, Massachusetts

These popcorn megaphones were a rage in 1958. Fans finished popcorn, knocked out the top and the bottom, and then used them to yell at the visiting team.

**Saturday afternoon
at Fenway Park.**

There's something special about the Boston area. When I made the big leagues, my hometown, Fall River [Massachusetts], tossed a day for me. I was a rookie. Who knew if I would stick with the Red Sox, or make it at all? But the fans were there for me, right at the start. They've been through a lot here and they stick with the ballclub.

—RUSS GIBSON, Boston Red Sox

are those teams that have a balanced attack and good defensive players," he mused. "Teams just don't get hot and win throughout a season. We have good pitching, good hitting, and some good fielders. The lineup is very solid, with people who've been playing a lot of baseball. It's the core of a good club. You never know what happens in a season. Who can predict anything in a game like this? I think it's a good club, though."

The players are full of enthusiasm. Greenwell, a genuine star who works hard to stay that way, lavishes praise on his teammates.

"Look at our lineup—that's a good hitting lineup," he observed, rubbing a knuckle over a slight shaving cut on his boyish face. "Boggs is a great hitter.... You've got power in that lineup, averages. You've some good clutch hitters here. It's a good lineup from number one through number nine. There's no weak spot. We hustle." His cap tilted up slightly on his forehead, Greenwell continued. "We have a deep, balanced pitching staff. I think it's the best in baseball. There's another thing, too: the tradition. This is a club with a great history. You can't play on it without someone, everyday, bringing up names like Joe Cronin and Ted Williams and Cy Young. That motivates a lot of younger guys. This is a solid team, a team that could

Manager Joe Morgan took over the Red Sox in mid-season in 1988 and helped turn them into one of the best teams in baseball in the late '80s and early '90s. He was released following a second-place finish in 1991.

win any day of the year, beat any team in the majors."

It's a team, too, as cherished by its fans as any team from the '60s, the '40s, or back into the mists of the teens when Babe Ruth pitched shutouts.

"The fans get emotional when the players get emotional," insists Rick Sachs, a longtime fan. "Lately, the Sox have become an emotional team. They are pumped up. I remember Dewey [Evans] hit two homers in one game [in 1990] and the whole team ran onto the field to hug him. You haven't seen that here in years. The fans went crazy. Those kind of players, the guys we have now, are going to make fans love them."

And it's a team full of players who know little of the historic jinx that has shadowed the Sox since 1918, players who couldn't care less about a jinx. "That stuff is from a long time ago, nobody pays much attention to that in the dugout," shrugged Greenwell. "Only writers remember that stuff."

Whatever the decade brings, it's certain to be full of excitement. Statistics and standings show that the team has been consistent over the last few years. The hitting is there, the pitching is there, the depth is there. The fan support is certainly there. The wait for a world championship has been a long one and the fans of New England have been patient, but it has to come and it has to come soon. And when the championships start to come, you know what's going to happen, don't you? From coast to coast everyone will be screaming, "Break Up the Red Sox!"

RED SOX GREATS

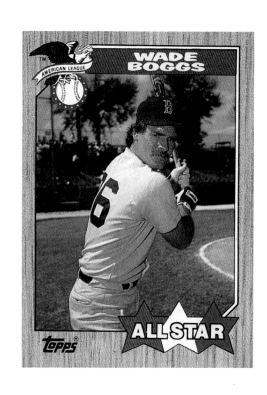

WADE BOGGS:

If anyone is going to hit .400 again, it'll be Wade Boggs. The uncannily consistent slugger has been hitting .340-plus during his eight-year career and can smack hard line-drive singles and doubles to any field.

Boggs has overcome criticism on his low home run figures, his fielding, and even his personal life to remain one of the game's top hitters. He is extremely superstitious, relying on a diet of chicken at nearly every meal and running sprints at the exact same time each night. It works.

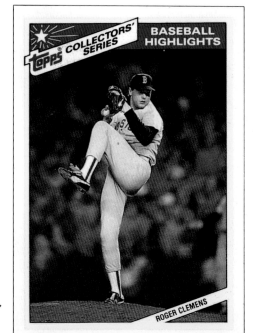

ROGER CLEMENS:

The "Rocket" is the best pitcher in baseball today, probably one of the best of all time. He has won back-to-back Cy Young awards, holds the all-time record of twenty strikeouts in one game, and has continued to dominate baseball like no American League pitcher since Whitey Ford.

The tall, muscular hurler has tremendous perseverance, a win-at-all-costs attitude, and an amazing ability to ignore off-field events that might overwhelm others. Despite a suspension following a dispute in the 1990 playoffs and a winter nightclub dispute, Clemens roared off to one of his best starts yet in 1991. He may wind up being the best Cy Young award winner the Red Sox have had since —well—Cy Young.

TONY CONIGLIARO:

Tony C. was a brave and tragic figure, a player New England fans can never forget. The casual, good-looking Conigliaro exploded on the baseball scene in 1964 with twenty-four home runs and a .290 batting average, only to break his arm in August. The next season he still managed to smash thirty-two home runs, but two years later he was hit in the face with a fastball and suffered severe damage. Conigliaro made a heroic comeback, returning to the lineup in 1969, but while he hit thirty-six home runs in 1971, he was never the same. A 1975 comeback failed and he was out of baseball.

A few years later, at the age of thirty-seven, Conigliaro's bad luck hit its peak. That year he suffered a heart attack, and after being bedridden for months he finally died.

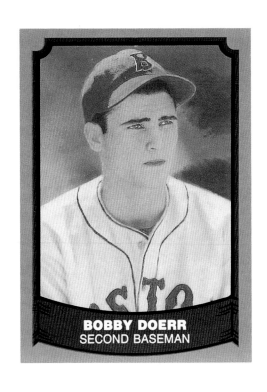

BOBBY DOERR
SECOND BASEMAN

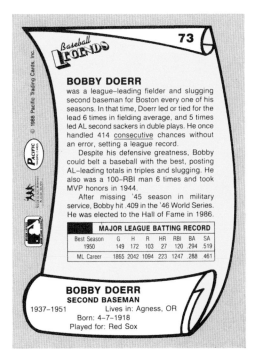

BOBBY DOERR:

The quiet second baseman never played for any team but the Red Sox and never hit below .270 in any season. He hit over .300 three times and in 1944 he led the league in slugging percentage. Doerr returned from military service in 1946 to help the team win the pennant, hitting a remarkable .409 during the World Series on top of that year's .271 average.

CARLTON FISK:

One of the greatest catchers in the history of the game, Fisk was the only American Leaguer selected unanimously as Rookie of the Year when he came up in 1972. That year he hit .293 with twenty-two home runs, the start of a long and productive career with the Red Sox through 1980. Following a contract dispute he joined the Chicago White Sox, with whom he continued to play well.

Fisk has played more games as a catcher than anyone else and hit more home runs as a catcher than anyone else. But he won't be remembered for that. As long as baseball is played in New England, Fisk will be remembered for "willing" fair his dramatic twelfth-inning home run in the sixth game of the 1975 World Series.

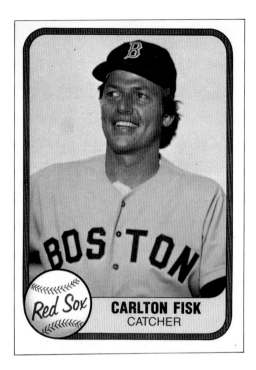

MIKE GREENWELL:

Just as Yaz had to step into Ted Williams's oversized shoes in left field, so has Greenwell stepped into Yaz's (via Jim Rice). He burst onto the diamond in 1987, smashing a home run in his first at-bat. That season he finished third in Rookie of the Year voting and in 1988 went on to hit .300. Greenwell, who has learned to play the Wall well, has been a consistent .300 hitter since he arrived in Boston.

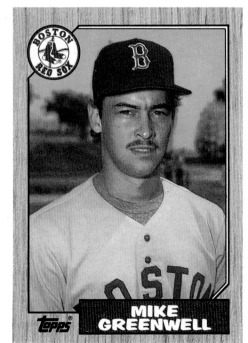

JOHNNY PESKY:

Shortstop Johnny Pesky joined the Red Sox with a sizzle, smashing 205 hits his rookie season in 1942 for a .331 average. He then spent three years in the service during World War II but rushed right back into the batter's box, posting a .335 average with 218 hits in 1946 and averaging .324 in 1947. Lifetime, he hit a solid .307.

Despite his extraordinary skill with a bat, Pesky is best remembered for an error. In the final game of the 1946 World Series he held a cut-off throw from the outfield too long and allowed Enos Slaughter to score, streaking all the way from first. The Sox lost the Series.

After retirement, Pesky spent several years managing the Sox and their farm clubs, later logging five years in the broadcast booth. Today, he is a familiar figure around Fenway and Boston as general manager Lou Gorman's assistant.

JIMMY PIERSALL:

During his first season with Boston in 1952 the eccentric Piersall suffered a nervous breakdown (memorialized in the film *Fear Strikes Out*), but then went on to a long fifteen-year career with a number of teams. Undaunted by his illness, Piersall played for the Red Sox from 1953 through 1958, hitting .293 in 1956 and later playing for the Washington Senators and the New York Mets.

Piersall was best known for his bizarre antics on the field. He once hid behind the monuments in Yankee Stadium while playing center field and ran the bases backwards when he hit his hundredth home run.

JIM RICE:

Jim Rice was always one of the Red Sox's finest players, dating from his sensational rookie season in 1975 when he averaged .309, hit twenty-two home runs, and posted 102 RBIs. Teammate Fred Lynn still beat him out for both Rookie of the Year and MVP, but Rice continued to play with great strength, becoming a powerful left fielder and hitting a career total of 382 home runs at Boston. Not until the late '70s did the moody fielder finally earn the appreciation he deserved when he clubbed forty-six home runs in 1978 and another thirty-nine in 1979. Perhaps Rice's best season came in 1986, however, when he led the Sox to a pennant by hitting .324, cracking 100 RBIs, and smacking twenty home runs.

SPEAKER Boston Amer.

PETE RUNNELS:

Although he played for the Washington Senators longer than the Red Sox, Runnels had a fine career with Boston, hitting .320 in 1960 to win the American League batting championship, following it up with a sensational .326 in 1962, and averaging over .300 for five straight seasons. He was also one of the most versatile infielders in baseball, splitting his career almost equally between first, second, and shortstop. Runnels returned to Boston in 1966 for a short-lived, sixteen-game career as manager.

TRIS SPEAKER:

Speaker was with the Red Sox for only seven of his twenty-two seasons in the majors but they were sensational years.

Arriving in Boston in 1907, he was soon hitting .340 regularly. He also became the game's best center fielder, revolutionizing the position by playing a very shallow center that enabled him to throw out runners at first and second. Teamed with Duffy Lewis and Harry Hooper, Speaker anchored baseball's best outfield from 1910 to 1915.

Lifetime, Speaker hit .344 with 1,881 RBIs. Later he became manager of the Cleveland Indians for seven seasons and led them to a world championship.

CARL YASTRZEMSKI

Height: 5'11" Weight: 188 Bats: Left Throws: Right Signed: Red Sox-1958, Prior to Draft
Acquired: Signed, Free Agent, 11-28-58. Born: 8-22-39, Southampton, N.Y. Home: Light House Point, Fla.

480

THE CIRCULAR METAL WEIGHT PLACED ON BATS IS CALLED A "DOUGHNUT."

COMPLETE MAJOR LEAGUE BATTING RECORD

Year	Club	G	AB	R	H	2B	3B	HR	RBI	AVG
1961	Red Sox	148	583	71	155	31	6	11	80	.266
1962	Red Sox	160	646	99	191	43	6	19	94	.296
1963	Red Sox	151	570	91	183	40	3	14	68	.321
1964	Red Sox	151	567	77	164	29	9	15	67	.289
1965	Red Sox	133	494	78	154	45	3	20	72	.312
1966	Red Sox	160	594	81	165	39	2	16	80	.278
1967	Red Sox	161	579	112	189	31	4	44	121	.326
1968	Red Sox	157	539	90	162	32	2	23	74	.301
1969	Red Sox	162	603	96	154	28	2	40	111	.255
1970	Red Sox	161	566	125	186	29	0	40	102	.329
1971	Red Sox	148	508	75	129	21	2	15	70	.254
1972	Red Sox	125	455	70	120	18	2	12	68	.264
1973	Red Sox	152	540	82	160	25	4	19	95	.296
1974	Red Sox	148	515	93	155	25	2	15	79	.301
1975	Red Sox	149	543	91	146	30	1	14	60	.269
1976	Red Sox	155	546	71	146	23	2	21	102	.267
Maj. Lea. Totals		2421	8848	1402	2559	489	50	338	1343	.289

* © 1977 TOPPS CHEWING GUM, INC. PRTD. IN U.S.A.

TED WILLIAMS:

When he tried out for his high school team, Williams hit a ball over a fence, over a parking lot, and onto the roof of the school. When he broke into the majors, in his first game as a rookie he smashed a double off one of the best pitchers in baseball, Red Ruffing, and hit .324 in his first season.

Williams's stats are amazing. He hit .344 lifetime with 521 home runs, even though he sat out five entire seasons while in the military. He led the league in hitting six times and in home runs six times. And to top it all off, he was the last man to hit .400. Williams went into Cooperstown in 1966.

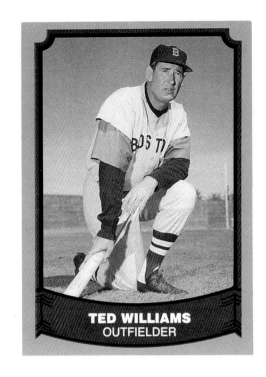

TED WILLIAMS
OUTFIELDER

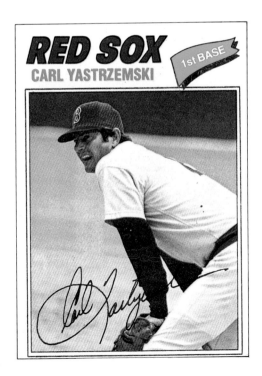

RED SOX 1st BASE
CARL YASTRZEMSKI

CARL YASTRZEMSKI:

When Ted Williams left the Red Sox, Yaz was introduced to his shoes and told to fill them—which he did. Although he started slowly and was never, ever, totally pleased with himself, Yastrzemski left baseball as one of the all-time greats. He hit .285 lifetime, crashed 452 home runs, and became the only American Leaguer with three thousand hits and four hundred home runs. He ranks first lifetime in games (3,308), third in both at-bats (11,988) and walks (1,845), sixth in total bases (5,539), and ninth in RBIs (1,844).

Yaz was an extremely competent outfielder who was still chasing fly balls at the age of forty-three. He played the tricky Green Monster like a magician, frequently standing casually in front of it, glove up, to fool runners into thinking he was about to catch a fly ball when he knew it would hit the wall. He was inducted into the Hall of Fame in 1989.

RED SOX STATS
RED SOX ALL-TIME PITCHING LEADERS

WINS
Young	193
Parnell	123
Tiant	122
Clemens	116
Wood	116
Stanley	115
Dobson	106
Grove	105
Hughson	96
Monbouquette	96
Lee	94
Brewer	91
Leonard	90
F. Sullivan	90
Ruth	89
Hurst	88
Kinder	86

ERA (1000 IP)
Wood	1.99
Young	2.00
Leonard	2.11
Ruth	2.19
Mays	2.21
Collins	2.51
Dinneen	2.81
Clemens	2.89
Winter	2.91
Hughson	2.94
Kinder	3.28
Grove	3.34
Tiant	3.36
S. Jones	3.39
F. Sullivan	3.47
Culp	3.50

WINNING PCT. (100 Dec.)
Clemens (116-51)	.695
Wood (116-56)	.674
Ruth (89-46)	.659
Hughson (96-54)	.640
Young (193-112)	.633
Grove (105-62)	.629
Kinder (86-52)	.623
Parnell (123-75)	.621
Tannehill (62-38)	.620
W. Ferrell (62-40)	.608
Tiant (122-81)	.601
Dobson (106-72)	.596
Leonard (90-63)	.588
Mays (72-51)	.585
Lee (94-68)	.580
Collins (84-62)	.575

SHUTOUTS
Young	38
Wood	28
Tiant	26
Clemens	25
Leonard	25
Parnell	20
Collins	19
Hughson	19
S. Jones	18
Dobson	17
Ruth	17
Dinneen	16
Monbouquette	16
G. Foster	15
Grove	15
Mays	14
F. Sullivan	14

LOSSES
Young	112
Stanley	97
Winter	97
Ruffing	96
Russell	94
Monbouquette	91
Dinneen	85
Brewer	82
Tiant	81
F. Sullivan	80
MacFayden	78
Parnell	75
Hurst	73
Dobson	72
Nixon	72
Delock	72

SAVES
Stanley	132
Radatz	104
Kinder	91
Lyle	69
Campbell	51
Fornieles	48
Drago	41
Burgmeier	40
Clear	38
Delock	31
Bolin	28
Kiely	28
Wyatt	28
Reardon	21
J. Wilson	20
Willoughby	20

INNINGS
Young	2728.1
Tiant	1774.0
Parnell	1752.2
Stanley	1707.0
Monbouquette	1622.0
Winter	1599.2
Dobson	1544.0
Grove	1539.2
Clemens	1513.0
Brewer	1509.1
F. Sullivan	1505.1
Lee	1504.0
Dinneen	1501.0
Hurst	1459.0
Wood	1418.0
Hughson	1375.2

COMPLETE GAMES
Young	275
Dinneen	156
Winter	141
Wood	121
Grove	119
Parnell	113
Tiant	113
Ruth	105
Hughson	99
Leonard	96
Collins	90
Dobson	90
Ehmke	83
W. Ferrell	81
Brewer	75
Ruffing	73
Monbouquette	72
F. Sullivan	72

GAMES
Stanley	637
Kinder	365
Young	327
Delock	322
Lee	321
Parnell	289
Fornieles	286
Radatz	286
Tiant	274
Lyle	260
Dobson	259
J. Wilson	258
Monbouquette	254
F. Sullivan	252
J. Russell	242

GAMES STARTED
Young	297
Tiant	238
Parnell	232
Monbouquette	228
Brewer	217
Hurst	217
Clemens	205
Dobson	202
F. Sullivan	201
Eckersley	191
Grove	189
Nixon	177
Winter	176
Dinneen	174
Lee	167

STRIKEOUTS
Clemens	1424
Young	1341
Tiant	1075
Hurst	1043
Wood	990
Monbouquette	969
F. Sullivan	821
Culp	794
Lonborg	784
Leonard	771
Grove	743
Brewer	733
Parnell	732
Eckersley	716
E. Wilson	714

RED SOX ALL-TIME BATTING LEADERS

BATTING AVG. (1500 AB)

Boggs	.346
T. Williams	.344
Speaker	.337
Foxx	.320
Runnels	.320
R. Johnson	.313
Pesky	.313
Lynn	.308
Goodman	.306
Cramer	.302
R. Ferrell	.302
Finney	.301
Cronin	.300
DiMaggio	.298
Rice	.298
McInnis	.296
J. Collins	.295

RUNS BATTED IN

Yastrzemski	1,844
T. Williams	1,839
Rice	1,451
Evans	1,346
Doerr	1,247
Foxx	788
Petrocelli	773
Cronin	737
Jensen	733
Malzone	716
D. Lewis	643
DiMaggio	618
Boggs	586
Speaker	570
Fisk	568
G. Scott	562
V. Stephens	562
R. Smith	536

HOME RUNS

T. Williams	521
Yastrzemski	452
Rice	382
Evans	379
Doerr	223
Foxx	222
Petrocelli	210
Jensen	170
T. Conigliaro	162
Fisk	162
G. Scott	154
R. Smith	149
Malzone	131
Lynn	124
V. Stephens	122
Cronin	119
Armas	113

EXTRA BASE HITS

Yastrzemski	1,157
T. Williams	1,117
Evans	925
Rice	834
Doerr	693
Boggs	469
Petrocelli	469
DiMaggio	452
Foxx	448
Cronin	433
Hooper	406
Fisk	402
Malzone	386
R. Smith	386
Speaker	386

RUNS

Yastrzemski	1,816
T. Williams	1,798
Evans	1,435
Rice	1,249
Doerr	1,094
DiMaggio	1,046
Hooper	988
Boggs	912
Pesky	776
Foxx	721
Speaker	704
Goodman	688
Petrocelli	653

DOUBLES

Yastrzemski	646
T. Williams	525
Evans	474
Doerr	381
Rice	373
Boggs	358
DiMaggio	308
Cronin	270
D. Lewis	254
Goodman	248
Hooper	246
Speaker	241
Petrocelli	237

GAMES

Yastrzemski	3,308
Evans	2,505
T. Williams	2,292
Rice	2,089
Doerr	1,865
Hooper	1,646
Petrocelli	1,553
DiMaggio	1,399
Malzone	1,359
Boggs	1,338
G. Scott	1,192
D. Lewis	1,184
Goodman	1,177
Cronin	1,134

STOLEN BASES

Hooper	300
Speaker	266
Yastrzemski	168
He. Wagner	141
L. Gardner	134
Parent	129
T. Harper	107
Werber	107
C. Stahl	105
J. Collins	102
D. Lewis	102
DiMaggio	100
Remy	98
Jensen	95
R. Smith	84

HITS

Yastrzemski	3,419
T. Williams	2,654
Rice	2,452
Evans	2,373
Doerr	2,042
Boggs	1,784
Hooper	1,707
DiMaggio	1,680
Malzone	1,454
Petrocelli	1,352
Goodman	1,344
Speaker	1,327
Pesky	1,277

TRIPLES

Hooper	130
Speaker	106
Freeman	91
Doerr	89
Gardner	87
Rice	79
Ferris	77
Evans	72
T. Williams	71
J. Collins	65
C. Stahl	64
Parent	63
D. Lewis	62

AT BATS

Yastrzemski	11,988
Evans	8,726
Rice	8,225
T. Williams	7,706
Doerr	7,093
Hooper	6,269
DiMaggio	5,640
Petrocelli	5,390
Malzone	5,273
Boggs	5,153
Goodman	4,399
D. Lewis	4,325
G. Scott	4,234
Pesky	4,085

RED SOX .300 SEASON HITTERS

Rank	Player	Avg.	Year	Rank	Player	Avg.	Year	Rank	Player	Avg.	Year
1.	T. Williams	.406	1941		J. Cronin	.325	1938		R. Smith	.309	1969
2.	T. Williams	.388	1957		J. Collins	.325	1902		B. Doerr	.309	1949
3.	T. Speaker	.383	1912	56.	J. Rice	.324	1986		S. Jolley	.309	1932
4.	D. Alexander	.372	1932		J. Pesky	.324	1947		T. Speaker	.309	1909
5.	T. Williams	.369	1948		B. Johnson	.324	1944	111.	M. Greenwell	.308	1989
6.	W. Boggs	.368	1985		J. Vosmik	.324	1938		J. Cronin	.308	1939
7.	W. Boggs	.366	1988		D. Pratt	.324	1921		L. Gardner	.308	1916
8.	W. Boggs	.363	1987	61.	E. Webb	.323	1930		G. Gessler	.308	1908
	T. Speaker	.363	1913	62.	P. Runnels	.322	1958	115.	J. Remy	.307	1981
10.	W. Boggs	.361	1983		W. Dropo	.322	1950		G. Kell	.307	1953
11.	J. Foxx	.360	1939		B Ruth	.322	1919		D. DiMaggio	.307	1949
12.	W. Boggs	.357	1986		T. Speaker	.322	1915		J. Cronin	.307	1937
13.	T. Williams	.356	1942	66.	D. Stapleton	.321	1980		B. Chapman	.307	1937
14.	B. Goodman	.354	1950		C. Yastrzemski	.321	1963		S. McInnis	.307	1921
15.	J. Foxx	.349	1938		B. Werber	.321	1934		D. Lewis	.307	1911
16.	B. Freeman	.346	1901	69.	J. Rice	.320	1977	122.	B. Goodman	.306	1952
17.	T. Williams	.345	1956		P. Runnels	.320	1960		J. Pesky	.306	1949
	T Williams	.345	1954		L. Finney	.320	1940		G. Burns	.306	1922
19.	T. Williams	.344	1940		R. Johnson	.320	1934		N. Leibold	.306	1921
20.	T. Williams	.343	1949	73.	T. Williams	.318	1951		F. Parent	.306	1901
	T. Williams	.343	1947		B. Doerr	.318	1939	127.	D. Evans	.305	1987
22.	T. Williams	.342	1946		C. Stahl	.318	1902		J. Rice	.305	1983
	P. Dougherty	.342	1902	76.	D. DiMaggio	.316	1946		D. Cramer	.305	1937
24.	B. Chapman	.340	1938		J. Harris	.316	1922		I. Flagstead	.305	1924
	T. Speaker	.340	1910	78.	J. Rice	.315	1978		S. McInnis	.305	1919
26.	J. Foxx	.338	1936		C. Fisk	.315	1977	132.	F. Parent	.304	1903
	T. Speaker	.338	1914		J. Jensen	.315	1956	133.	E. Burks	.303	1989
28.	C. Lansford	.336	1981		P. Fox	.315	1944		M. Barrett	.303	1984
29.	J. Pesky	.335	1946		R. Johnson	.315	1935		R. Smith	.303	1973
	J. Harris	.335	1923		L. Gardner	.315	1912		R. Smith	.303	1970
31.	T. Speaker	.334	1911	84.	F. Lynn	.314	1976		G. Scott	.303	1967
32.	F. Lynn	.333	1979		P. Runnels	.314	1959		B. Goodman	.303	1954
	E. Webb	.333	1931	86.	M. Easler	.313	1984		D. Cramer	.303	1940
	I. Boone	.333	1924		B. Goodman	.313	1953		M. Higgins	.303	1938
35.	F. Lynn	.331	1975		J. Pesky	.313	1951		C. Reynolds	.303	1934
	J. Pesky	.331	1942		R. Johnson	.313	1933		K. Williams	.303	1928
	P. Dougherty	.331	1903		B. Myer	.313	1928	143.	S. Mele	.302	1947
38.	W. Boggs	.330	1989		D. Prothro	.313	1925		M. Higgins	.302	1937
	I. Boone	.330	1925	92.	C. Yastrzemski	.312	1965		D. Lewis	.302	1917
40.	C. Yastrzemski	.329	1970		J. Pesky	.312	1950	146.	C. Lansford	.301	1982
	J. Collins	.329	1901		R. Ferrell	.312	1936		F. Lynn	.301	1980
42.	M. Greenwell	.328	1987		J. Hodapp	.312	1933		C. Yastrzemski	.301	1974
	T. Williams	.328	1958		H. Hooper	.312	1920		C. Yastrzemski	.301	1968
	D. DiMaggio	.328	1950	97.	J. Cronin	.311	1941		D. DiMaggio	.301	1940
	G. Burns	.328	1923		D. Cramer	.311	1939		D. Cramer	.301	1938
46.	T. Williams	.327	1939		H. Hooper	.311	1911		R. Ferrell	.301	1935
47.	C. Yastrzemski	.326	1967		H. Lord	.311	1909		J. Harris	.301	1924
	P. Runnels	.326	1962		B. Freeman	.311	1902		D. Pratt	.301	1922
49.	M. Greenwell	.325	1988		C. Stahl	.311	1901	155.	J. Foxx	.300	1941
50.	W. Boggs	.325	1984	103.	M. Vernon	.310	1956		M. Menosky	.300	1921
	J. Rice	.325	1979		B. Goodman	.310	1948		J. Rothrock	.300	1929
	A. Zarilla	.325	1950	105.	J. Rice	.309	1982				
	B. Doerr	.325	1944		J. Rice	.309	1975				

BIBLIOGRAPHY

Clemens, Roger, with Peter Gammons. *Rocket Man: The Roger Clemens Story*. Lexington, Mass.: S. Greene Press, 1987.

Coleman, Ken, and Dan Valentine. *The Impossible Dream Remembered: The '67 Red Sox*. Lexington, Mass.: S. Greene Press, 1980.

Frommer, Harvey. *Baseball's Greatest Rivalry: The New York Yankees vs. the Boston Red Sox*. New York: Atheneum Publishers, 1982.

Higgins, George V. *The Progress of the Season: Forty Years of Baseball in Our Town*. New York: Henry Holt & Co., 1989.

Hirshberg, Al. *What's the Matter with the Red Sox?* Boston: Dodd Mead, 1973.

Honig, Donald. *The Boston Red Sox: An Illustrated Tribute*. New York: St. Martin's Press, 1984.

Jaspersohn, William. *The Ballpark: One Day Behind the Scenes*. Boston: Little, Brown & Co., 1980.

Shaughnessy, Dan. *The Curse of the Bambino*. New York: E. P. Dutton, 1990.

Yastrzemski, Carl, and Gerlad Eskenazi. *Yaz: Baseball, the World and Me*. New York: Doubleday, 1990.

AUTOGRAPH PAGES

127

INDEX

129

PHOTOGRAPHY CREDITS